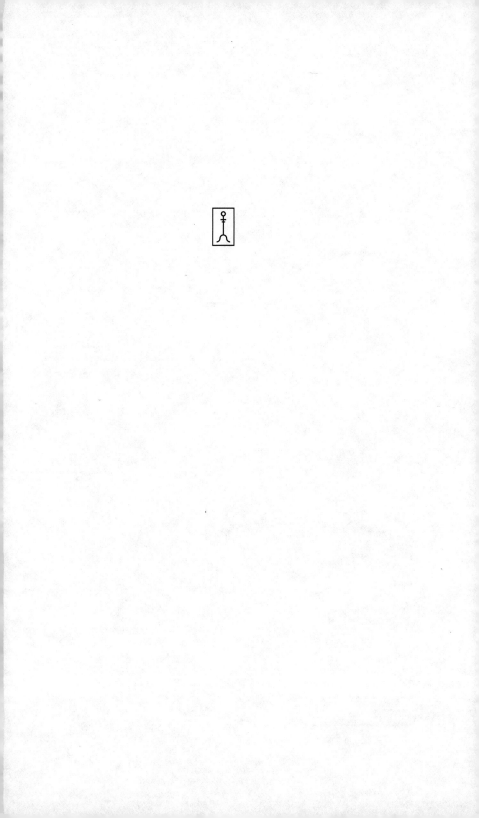

OTHER BOOKS BY LAURA DOYLE

The Surrendered Wife
The Surrendered Single

THE SUPERWOMAN'S PRACTICAL GUIDE
TO GETTING AS MUCH AS SHE GIVES

Things Will Get As GOOD *As You Can* STAND

*(...when you learn that it is
better to receive than to give)*

LAURA DOYLE

A FIRESIDE BOOK
PUBLISHED BY SIMON & SCHUSTER
New York   London   Toronto   Sydney

All the names have been changed in the stories in this book, to protect privacy. Some of the circumstances have been changed for simplicity.

FIRESIDE
Rockefeller Center
1230 Avenue of the Americas
New York, NY 10020

FIRESIDE and colophon are registered trademarks
of Simon & Schuster, Inc.

For information about special discounts for bulk purchases,
please contact Simon & Schuster Special Sales at
1-800-456-6798 or business@simonandschuster.com.

Designed by Jan Pisciotta

Manufactured in the United States of America

1   3   5   7   9   10   8   6   4   2

Library of Congress Cataloging-in-Publication Data
Doyle, Laura.
Things will get as good as you can stand : —when you learn that it is better to receive than to give : the superwoman's practical guide to getting as much as she gives / Laura Doyle.
p.   cm.
"Fireside book."
1. Women—Life skills guides. 2. Women—Conduct of life. 3. Women—Psychology. I. Title: Superwoman's practical guide to getting as much as she gives. II. Title.
HQ1221.D7 2004
646.7'082—dc22   2003070407
ISBN 978-0-7432-4515-9

For women everywhere
who could use more rest, play, and solitude.
May you get as much as you give!

ACKNOWLEDGMENTS

I couldn't have completed this book without the wisdom, truth telling, encouragement, laughter, and organizational skills of my editors: Doris Cooper and Christine Gordon. Every time we work on a book together it just makes me feel closer and more affectionate toward both of them, and remember how brilliant they are. I'm grateful for the wonderful gift of their talents applied to my writing.

I'm also grateful for the steady support of Jimmy Vines, my agent. He is truly one of the good guys.

London King and Marcia Burch are amazingly talented women who have exceeded my expectations in helping me get the word out, and they are a joy to work with. I'm so fortunate to have their expertise and enthusiasm.

Part of the reason I'm such a great receiver is because I have a very generous group of friends who keep me in good practice: Nan Johnson, Greg Kishida, Kolleen Mayou, Robin Rios, Tom Rotter, Les Takemeto, and Len Tullgren.

Special thanks to my husband, John Doyle, who keeps taking me higher through his unwavering devotion. I can accomplish the things I do today largely because I've had fourteen years to see myself through his eyes. What a gift!

Contents

Chapter 12
Say What You Want

Chapter 13
Admit That You Goofed and
Apologize for Your Part

INTRODUCTION

> *The human race has had a long experience and a fine tradition in surviving adversity. But we now face a task for which we have little experience, the task of surviving prosperity.*
>
> —ALAN GREGG

WOMEN REJECT THE VERY THINGS THEY SAY THEY WANT THE MOST

YEARS AGO SOME FRIENDS offered to treat my husband, John, and me to dinner for our wedding anniversary. As we were preparing for the evening, I started to fret. "Now we have to find out when *their* anniversary is so we can take *them* out to dinner," I said to John.

I wasn't thinking about how much fun we would have with our friends, and I wasn't grateful for their thoughtfulness. Instead I turned their gift into a debt that would have to be paid.

But John had a wise response. "Did you ever think that just having your company at dinner is enough and that you don't owe them anything besides that?"

The idea that I could relish a gift without worrying about reciprocating was new to me.

⁂

Accepting what someone offered simply for my enjoyment made me uncomfortable. Dinners. Theater tickets that a friend couldn't use. A bottle of wine from houseguests. Neighborly offers such as a ride to pick up my car or the favor of rescuing our mail while John and I were away. A birthday phone call. Anything that was meant to bring me joy or to make my life a little easier and nicer would flood me with anxiety and a suffocating sense of obligation.

And I'm not the only one. One woman described feeling stressed out when her husband invited her for a romantic Friday night dinner. Accepting his invitation meant she had to focus to finish her work, call a baby-sitter (and clean the house before the sitter arrived), and get the kids fed and bathed. Not only that, she figured that her husband would want to have sex with her after they came home—when she knew she would be exhausted.

Ah. Superwoman Syndrome in its purest form.

This woman could have asked her husband, the baby-sitter (who is paid to feed and bathe children), and even her oldest child for some help instead of doing everything herself as if she were a superwoman. She could have kept the perspective that her husband just wanted to show her a good time instead of feeling obligated to him.

Like me, she had a hard time receiving without feeling indebted.

Favor offering and repaying and gift giving and receiving were column headings on a giant scorecard I kept in my head, and I never wanted to lag behind. Worrying that I wouldn't be able to afford to reciprocate heightened my distress.

All that anxiety and worry was the knife that severed my connections with the people who loved and cared about me. Ultimately, my incessant rejecting of gifts—whether they came wrapped with a bow, arrived in the form of favors and help, or appeared as kind words uttered just when I needed a pick-me-up—signaled to my friends and family that their offers weren't welcome. Eventually, they dried up. And so did the friendships.

When I said that I didn't need help after a dinner party or claimed that I really was in need of a haircut when someone complimented me on my appearance, I was unwittingly keeping my friendships at arm's length. My friends didn't see me as independent and self-sufficient but rather as someone who, in rejecting their offers, was rejecting them.

I felt alone. Without support and the warmth of hearing that I was beautiful or had done something well, my self-esteem flagged. And I was completely exhausted because I had trapped myself in a corner where I had to do everything single-handedly. I didn't realize that I was rejecting the very things that I—and every woman I know—wanted most: more time, help, understanding, prosperity, and validation.

I didn't realize my isolation was self-imposed—I just thought life was overwhelming.

> *All of us at certain moments of our lives need to take advice*
> *and to receive help from other people.*
>
> ALEXIS CARREL

I THOUGHT I WAS SUPERWOMAN

Feeling as if I had to be a superwoman who didn't need anything from anybody also put a strain on my marriage because I didn't know how to receive from my husband. When he offered to take me away for the weekend, I argued that we couldn't afford it. Instead of showing gratitude when he washed the dishes, I found fault with his work and mumbled that I could have done it better myself, which discouraged him from helping the next time. I said, "That's okay" when he offered to make dinner because I figured I could do it faster. After I snarled, "Yeah, right" when he told me that I looked great before an important meeting, he stopped complimenting me. Then I was mad because I felt unnoticed and unappreciated.

What a mess.

And that's not all. I felt guilty when I was relaxing or doing something I loved, like walking along the beach or buying a new pair of shoes, because not only was I intolerant of other people's kindness, but I hadn't yet developed a tolerance for treating myself well. Instead, I worked long hours at a job I hated because that felt useful and important, even though it didn't make me happy.

No wonder I was always cranky.
I am a reformed poor receiver.

Our dilemma is that we hate change and love it at the same time; what we really want is for things to remain the same but get better.

—SYDNEY J. HARRIS

WHAT TO DO WHEN THE EASY TIMES HIT

Most people know what to do when tough times hit—circle the wagons, hunker down, and try to get through as best you can. If tomorrow is the big deadline for a project that's not ready, you'd probably make a pot of coffee and plan to work through the wee hours. If money's suddenly tight, you ration what you have for groceries and other necessities. If you lose your job, you network like crazy until you get another one. When the goal is survival, it's not hard to figure out what to do next, and you don't feel guilty about it. But when you suddenly have a free afternoon with no responsibilities, get a nicer car than you've ever had, attract an amazing guy who falls in love with you, or get promoted over three people who have been at the company longer, what do you do?

You try to enjoy it, of course.

But that can be tricky.

I knew one couple who lived meagerly until they received

a substantial inheritance. Before long, they had spent it and returned to their paltry lifestyle. They understood how to struggle, but they had not developed a tolerance for living much beyond that. Having extra money didn't fit with their picture of themselves, so they unconsciously returned to their low but familiar standard of living. We do the same thing with gifts.

When I first became self-employed, I was so used to working from eight A.M. to five P.M. Monday through Friday that I felt as though I wasn't working hard if I slept in on a Tuesday. No one but me was expecting me to get up at a certain time, and I had never been a morning person, but my Protestant work ethic dictated that I should stick to that familiar schedule. If I stayed up late at night writing, I judged myself harshly for being undisciplined and not getting my work done in the morning. I wasn't focused on my excellent productivity (I was writing two books) but rather on the fact that I was abusing the privilege of being self-employed.

Now I recognize that I enjoy writing at night—I feel alert and rested in the evening, and there are fewer interruptions. I've finally developed a tolerance for something that's really great for me—the ability to set my own work hours.

But it wasn't easy.

We have to reprogram ourselves to be comfortable with more love, free time, success, confidence, money, or a situation that is better than we already have, but it can be done.

Receiving is the key.

If you limit your choices only to what seems possible or reasonable, you disconnect yourself from what you truly want, and all that is left is a compromise.

—ROBERT FRITZ

YOU'LL FEEL AS IF YOU'RE GETTING AWAY WITH SOMETHING

Focusing on being a good receiver will help you override any temptation to dismiss or reject the things that you say you want but that you can't seem to get. Chances are, having them makes you feel uncomfortable. In other words, when you change your behavior to become a good receiver—when you tolerate having what is good and pleasurable for you—you will have more peace in your life. If you're like me, you'll feel delight and surprise that life can be so easy.

When you discover the bounty of time, love, and everything else that is good that comes as a direct result of receiving, you increase your capacity for more wonderful, surprising, exciting, tender things to happen to you.

Learning to receive will at first be unfamiliar and uncomfortable. But this book will show you how to ride out the awkwardness.

In the following pages you will learn simple, practical steps that will help you make receiving your habit. You will learn how to choose confidence and graciousness over insecurity and guilt. As a result, your romantic relationship, friendships, and family connections will be more intimate and enjoyable. You'll have more free time and less stress, and you'll develop an acceptance—a tolerance—for what you want but have unconsciously rejected in the past because you didn't think you were deserving.

When you master the art of receiving graciously, magical things happen. Instead of doing the dishes by yourself the morning after the party, you have a splash-fest with the friend who stayed late to help you clean the kitchen. Leisure time becomes more abundant. Instead of having leftovers and watching TV on Friday night, you let someone take you to a romantic dinner and a movie. Compliments you would have dismissed serve to make you feel more confident, and you connect more deeply with loved ones.

Adopting the habits of a gracious receiver will help you draw things to you with minimal effort instead of struggling to pull them toward you by force or manipulation. Becoming a gracious receiver will also make you more attractive. If you learn to receive, you'll have more energy to devote to the things you've always wanted to do—learning French, cultivating a garden, getting in shape, taking care of a child, or running a corporation.

All of this will happen just as soon as you discover and develop your receiving muscles, so keep reading.

Chapter 1

✦

HOW I DISCOVERED MY RECEIVING MUSCLES, AND HOW YOU CAN, TOO

Maybe you don't reject the things that you're offered—or perhaps you do so without realizing it. Make it your mission to identify ways you might have rejected things that were offered for your enjoyment. The world is an abundant place, so anything we're lacking in our lives very often reflects an area where we aren't yet receiving.

Notice if you feel guilty or anxious when someone compliments you or tries to help you, but don't mention it to them.

When I'm trusting and being myself . . . everything in my life reflects this by falling into place easily, often miraculously.

—SHAKTI GAWAIN

I WAS STANDING IN MY OWN WAY

TURNING DOWN OFFERS that were meant to delight me hurt me in more ways than one. The guilt and control that were stiffening my receiving muscles took the biggest toll on my marriage. I didn't recognize this until after one particularly awful night. John announced that he was taking me out but wouldn't say where we were going. He said that he wanted to give me a special treat and that I should just relax and enjoy the surprise that was coming my way.

Unfortunately, I had no idea how to do that.

First I badgered John to tell me where we were going, but he wouldn't budge. When we arrived at a familiar restaurant, I told him where to park so that we would be able to get out and avoid the postdinner car congestion. Next I asked him if he had enough money on him to cover the cost of dinner. When John tried to pull out my chair for me, I ignored him and pulled it out myself. When the bill came, I told John what I thought he should leave for a tip. When we left the restaurant, John tried to take me to the movies, but because the evening had been out of my control, I was so anxious that I just wanted to go home.

You can imagine the jerkiness of the evening. Every time John did something, I put on the brakes. Being with me was like driving a car that's stuck in first gear. Far from being romantic and fun, it was exhausting and stressful.

Unwittingly, I had sabotaged John's efforts at creating a sweet, intimate evening.

I'm embarrassed to admit that I had no idea how to just enjoy myself while I was being treated to a night out. I couldn't stand not calling the shots. Being in control made me feel secure.

And, being surprised—even pleasantly—made me anxious.

I Had the Kookiest Problem

At home, I took a hot bath to soothe myself. Sitting in the tub, I struggled to figure out why I couldn't enjoy myself on a night out with my husband. I tried to think of something besides me that was wrong with the evening, but I couldn't.

I was the problem. I realized then that if I ever wanted to have intimacy with my husband—who loved me and wanted me to be happy—I would have to learn to ride out the initial discomfort of being in the spotlight.

I would have to find the courage to receive graciously.

That night I discovered that my capacity for enjoyment was limited. The only thing standing between me and my having romantic nights out with my husband was the discomfort I experienced when I was treated well. Prior to that night, I figured that the problem was with my husband, or that we couldn't afford to go out, or that marriage isn't like dating. But seeing John try so hard to make the evening special and to plan it with all the things he knew I loved, and watching myself systematically reject his efforts, made me realize that I was blocking my own pleasure. It was like knowing that Ed McMahon was at the door with a sweepstakes check and not opening it because I wasn't sure how much money I would get.

If I wanted good times—let alone intimacy—with my husband and others, I was going to have to increase my *tolerance* for good treatment.

Looking back, I can see how I had been turning down gifts and special treatment my whole life, but it wasn't until that night that I had my "aha" moment. In that flash of clarity I felt as though I had the kookiest problem in the world and that no one else would understand it. I didn't know of any books or advice columns or talk-show hosts who'd ever talked about *receiving*.

I had no idea how I would begin to change, but I knew I had to do something because I desperately wanted to stop blocking all the kindnesses, treats, and even money that could come my way. I racked my brain for ways to overcome my anxiety. Then, one afternoon while I was quietly folding laundry on my bed, I remembered what I had learned from singing in front of an audience.

For my first performance—a gig at a tiny coffeehouse in the suburbs of Los Angeles—I had been so nervous and self-conscious that I didn't enjoy myself at all. I spent the whole night wincing internally at my mistakes, and I was one big pretzel when the show was over. But I didn't let that stop me from coming back to perform again the next week, and, when nobody said anything about how awful I was, I felt a little less anxious. Over time and dozens of gigs, I grew so comfortable being on stage that I actually enjoyed myself. Eventually, I stopped thinking about the mistakes and just had fun connecting with the audience by smiling at them and singing their requests.

I decided that I would make myself accept as much good treatment as possible, just the way I decided to keep performing on stage despite my sweaty palms and pounding chest. I put myself on a receiving regimen, hoping to improve the intimacy in my marriage, deepen my friendships, improve my standard of living, and simply make myself into someone our neighbors and community thought was pleasant and gracious. I made my mantra "receive, receive, receive!" I hoped that if I got used to good treatment, I would eventually begin to enjoy it.

Little did I know that would also attract more to me.

I Had to Override the Alarm System in My Head

FORCING MYSELF TO SAY nothing but "thank you" to John's compliments and the nice things he would do when I was least expecting them—even if I thought they were undeserved—was as uncomfortable as using muscles I hadn't stretched in years. But the more I used those receiving muscles, the more confident I grew from hearing—and believing—compliments that I once would have dismissed.

When John offered to do the dishes, I ignored my fears that he would leave streaks on the glasses and said only "thank you," so I could have a little time to myself after dinner to read a book or chat on the phone with my friends. My receiving muscles grew stronger, and I experienced a calmness I had never felt in the days when I was frazzled from doing everything myself. I felt prettier and smarter and more loved because John was constantly telling me how beautiful, intelligent, and beloved I was now that I was no longer rebuffing his kind words.

When you hear something enough times, you start to believe it, and hearing and believing how wonderful and adored I was gave me ongoing incentive to receive.

Before I knew it, receiving graciously had become second nature. I started flexing my new muscles outside of the house and in every area of my life. One day I let the box boy carry a single bag of groceries to the car for me, which I had never done because I thought it was too indulgent. I imagined that other people were wondering what was wrong with the able-bodied woman who couldn't even carry her own groceries to the car. But I didn't see any strange, critical looks (and trust me, I was searching for them), and the box boy didn't seem to mind one bit, so I did it again the next week. Eventually, I noticed that I didn't dread the trip to the supermarket anymore: one of the things I hated most about shopping—lugging bags to the car—had disappeared.

At work, when a coworker praised me in front of two

other people, I worried that word would spread that I was conceited for saying nothing but "thank you." But if word did spread, it never got back to me.

I received an apology from a friend whose beater car leaked oil in our driveway. I didn't say, "That's okay," and secretly resent her for her jalopy. I just said, "Thanks for that. Apology accepted." Hearing myself saying "thank you" so much made me realize I was receiving a lot. I felt grateful.

I was no longer rejecting the things I said I wanted more of—I was enjoying them. Things were getting good, and although I was uncomfortable at times, I could stand it.

The deepest principle in human nature is the craving to be appreciated.

—WILLIAM JAMES

How I Know It's Better to Receive Than to Give

THEN CAME THE HOLIDAYS, and a friend presented me with a neatly wrapped box and a sly smile on her face. At first I was nervous because I had no present for her, but she didn't seem to care because she was so focused on her excitement over giving me a gift. She explained, "This reminded me so much of you I just had to get it." I laughed when I opened the package to find a shirt that read BLONDE COMET beneath a picture of a cartoon blonde with her dukes up. We both laughed at how appropriate it was because the cartoon had my coloring and seemed to represent perfectly my spunky personality. We had a great time laughing together when I posed with my fists in the air like the girl on the T-shirt and said, "That's me!" That was all she needed in return.

I resisted the urge to go out and buy her something for the holidays. I knew I had also given her something by simply receiving and enjoying the present. Wrapping up a scarf for her at the last minute out of guilt would only have diminished her gift to me, which clearly came from a place of fun and inspiration rather than obligation. Instead, we both got a kick out of her present, especially when she saw me wearing it, which I did until it wore out.

That's when I learned that it's better to receive than to give.

ANYONE CAN LEARN TO RECEIVE

KNOWING HOW TO GIVE is important, and most women are wonderful givers. But we can't be good friends, wives, mothers, colleagues, and sisters without also learning to receive.

What's magical about receiving is that you find you have more free time as you let loved ones help you decorate for the party or write your résumé—even if you think you could have done those things yourself.

Your confidence will soar as you come to take in all the help, praise, and material gifts that people around you want to give you. Your receptivity will show you that you deserve them.

Take Victoria: When she acknowledged her secret desire to be an actress, the only person she felt safe enough to tell was her sister. To her surprise, her sister was supportive of Victoria's dream and offered to let her stay at her apartment on the nights she had acting class nearby. Just receiving that gesture of validation gave her the confidence to take a course that she had only fantasized about taking for years. The last time I spoke to Victoria, she had an agent and an impressive demo reel. To say her confidence had improved is an understatement.

You'll also feel more self-respect when you stop dismissing and start receiving apologies, because as you do, you'll realize that you deserve to have others keep their commitments to you and treat you thoughtfully.

Most important, your friendships and love relationships will grow stronger and more intimate as you become a gracious receiver. That's because receiving requires vulnerability, which in turn creates closeness born from a sense of trust. Good receivers know that they are also giving something when they simply let someone else please them.

No matter how strong your knee-jerk reactions are to appear modest and fend for yourself, you can start having the things you say you want the most—if you strengthen your receiving muscles.

Cats seem to go on the principle that it never does any harm to ask for what you want.

—JOSEPH WOOD KRUTCH

REFLECT ON WHAT YOU REJECT

IF YOU'RE LIKE I WAS, you may not even be aware that you're rejecting gifts. Maybe you just have a hard time simply saying "thank you" and taking in the kind words when someone pays you a compliment. When a friend says, "I'll get it," and grabs the check at lunch, you insist on paying your share because you don't want to burden your friend with the cost of the check—or feel that you now owe her something. When a coworker offers to carry one of the boxes of office supplies up the stairs, you might say, "That's okay—I've got it," to show that you're capable.

We tell ourselves we are just being efficient, considerate, and modest when someone is giving us something. Whatever the "reason" for rejecting gifts and compliments, the result is the same: you're rejecting things that are meant to give you pleasure and enjoyment.

Here's a quiz to help you identify the ways you might be inadvertently rejecting the things you say you want:

ARE YOU A GRACIOUS RECEIVER?

	Rarely	Sometimes	Frequently
1. When a friend apologizes for being twenty minutes late to meet you, you relieve the tension as quickly as possible by saying, "That's okay."			
2. When you find yourself wanting to have something that's unrealistic, you put it out of your mind so you won't set yourself up for disappointment.			
3. After a dinner party, two friends offer to stay and help you clean up. You say, "You don't have to do that."			
4. You've always known your hair is too thin, so when a coworker tells you that you have beautiful hair, you tell her thanks but point out that it's actually limp.			
5. When it comes to answering the question "What do you want to do tonight?" you hope that your partner or someone else will come up with a plan because you can never think of anything.			
6. You're a really busy person.			
7. You talked your best friend into making an investment that completely bombed. Of course she is unhappy about it and tension is high. You apologize repeatedly because you feel so guilty about it.			

	Rarely	Sometimes	Frequently
8. If someone asked you to name a part of your body that's gorgeous, it would take a while for you to come up with an answer.			
9. Your hate your job.			
10. You would feel uncomfortable letting someone support you financially.			

To total your score, give yourself:

- *5 points for each "rarely"*
- *3 points for each "sometimes"*
- *1 point for each "frequently"*
- *Add all three columns together for a final score (somewhere between 10 and 50)*

TOTAL POINTS: _____

If your score is 25 or less:

Life Doesn't Have to Be So Hard

It's not easy to be you, because although you're strong and hardworking, you're tired and often overwhelmed. Nobody looks her best when she's running ragged, but that's probably the least of your concerns at the moment. Mostly you'd like to know how to keep life from overtaking you completely. The good news is that an easier life, better relationships, and more free time are well within reach. For simple instructions on how to get off this treadmill and live the way you've always wanted to, read on.

If your score is 26–42:

The Good Life Is Just Around the Corner

You know how to take a compliment, and you wouldn't reject a present, but you sure could use some assistance. Stress is part of life, but you don't have to carry it all by yourself. That gray dullness you feel is a distinct lack of adequate fun. Sure, you're having some, but you could be having so much more. Read on and you'll see how.

If your score is more than 42:

Congratulations, You Relaxed, Confident Woman

You don't need me to tell you that life is good. You count your blessings every day, and the list is long. People are drawn to you because you're gracious and self-assured. You work hard, but you have time to yourself, wonderful support from family and friends, and plenty of fun and relaxation. This book will show you how to benefit even more from what you already do so well naturally.

Anyone can become a good receiver by following a few simple suggestions. But this book can help you start living the principle that it's better to receive than to give only if you first become conscious of your present behaviors and then replace them with new ones. In other words, begin to receive.

Chapter 2

❦

BEGIN TO RECEIVE

Notice how you feel when someone else doesn't receive from you. That sting—however slight—is the same rejection others feel from you when you dismiss or rebuff their gifts.

For one week, take note of everything you are offered each day. An offer could be anything from a sweet smile to a positive comment, from the glass of water that your husband brings you in bed to a spontaneous invitation to join your friend and her husband for dinner. Notice the offers that make you most uncomfortable. You may feel awkward, but you don't have to let on. Just practice saying "thank you" and nothing more.

The giving and receiving of pleasure is a need and an ecstasy.

—KAHLIL GIBRAN

MISS MANNERS WOULD NOT APPROVE, GENTLE READER

FORGET WHAT YOU'VE LEARNED about trying to appear modest. Receiving with grace means you take whatever is offered to you with ease and kindness. To be graceful is to be polite. And to be polite when you've been offered anything from a glass of water to dinner at an expensive restaurant means accepting that offer with thanks.

Why?

Because to reject a gift is to reject the giver.

Imagine that you are about to give your best office buddy an elegant but mysterious-looking bag, overstuffed with tissue. She's been having a tough time at work, and you want her to know that you've been thinking about her, so you buy her a gift certificate for a manicure and pedicure and put it in the big bag. You hope that you'll be able to brighten her spirits with a little pampering. Driving to work in the morning, you are remarkably energized—and happy to be going into the office. It's exciting to do something nice for someone else. You are looking forward to making her day. You hope that your gift will show her that you think she's a wonderful person and that you support her through her rough time. With great anticipation, you present her with the gift bag. She sighs as she opens it and keeps saying, "You shouldn't have."

When she gets beneath all the pastel-colored tissue, her face drops and she says, "You really didn't need to do this."

Where does that leave you?

Crestfallen, I suspect. You say, "I know, but I wanted to." But now you're wondering why you wanted to because not only didn't you get the satisfaction of seeing her face light up, you now feel awkward. All you were hoping for was to see her happy for a few minutes—to know that you brightened her day—but her gloomy response makes you feel as if *you've* failed. She seems more unhappy than she was before you gave her the gift. What a waste.

See how important it is to receive graciously?

You reject your best friend when you argue with her after she says you look beautiful. She wants the pleasure of giving you compliments—just as you want the joy of watching your friend open an elaborately wrapped gift in happy anticipation.

Receiving graciously is charming. It makes us more attractive and likable when we accept a friend's extra theater ticket, or smile warmly when she acknowledges how wonderful it is to receive a gift certificate to a spa out of the blue because it reflects a vulnerability—a very human part of us that's appealing. It lets others know that they can make us happy—that we know we're not completely self-sufficient. Letting someone else have the satisfaction of making your day makes her feel good—and you look good. When you accept a present, you have to acknowledge (at least momentarily) that you're worthy of it, even if you've done nothing to earn it.

And all you have to do to be worthy of something is to overcome any feelings of guilt or self-consciousness that would make you refuse a gift.

Those who cannot tell what they desire or expect, still sigh and struggle with indefinite thoughts and vast wishes.
—Ralph Waldo Emerson

Things Were Better Than I Could Stand

If you don't receive graciously, you send the message that you're not worthy, and others will perceive you that way.

If you act graciously even when you feel uncomfortable, you send the message that you know you're worthy.

That's what I had to do when friends of ours arranged for John and me to have not just an anniversary dinner, but an anniversary *weekend*. I knew that my choices were either to accept and enjoy the adventure or reject their well-planned gift. I admit that I felt some pangs of guilt that they had gone to such trouble and expense for us, but I didn't let on or indulge those feelings. Instead of fretting while six friends toasted us over a lavish brunch and then dropped us off at a beach resort for an overnight stay, I remember delighting in every minute of the experience—and also crying because I felt so loved. I was completely out of control because I had no say in where they were taking us (they had us blindfolded in the backseat) or how much they were spending (a lot). It was the kind of thrill you can have only from being out of control but knowing that you're in safe hands. Nothing I could have arranged myself would have been half as wonderful or made anyone—not me, not John, not my friends—as happy.

I let my friends know how amazed and delighted I was. "This is the best anniversary gift I can imagine," I told them. "What a great surprise. You guys outdid yourselves and you've made us very, very happy."

"Yeah—thanks a lot, you guys. This is fantastic," John added.

Our friends broke out in grins and were high-fiving one another. I could tell by their smiles and chatter that they were just as happy as we were—and having just as much fun. Their surprise was a hit and they felt appreciated for their creativity and effort.

Whether I did so out of modesty, self-sufficiency, or the feeling of being undeserving, I now know that I was rejecting gifts so I could stay in control. But rejecting the gift is rejecting the giver, which puts distance between me and the people I love. So unless I give up some control by accepting the discomfort and anxiety of receiving, there can be no intimacy. When I do relax into the pleasure of receiving a gift I feel the sweetness of emotional connection. I'm not completely self-sufficient, and I don't need to be. I was never meant to be.

Receiving is, after all, the best gift.

> *If you see no reason for giving thanks, the fault lies in your-self.*
>
> —Native American proverb

Get Glad, Not Even

Another form of trying to stay in control is to keep the score even by giving a compliment when you get one. For example, when a friend says how much she likes your shoes, you immediately find something to praise about her appearance. Instead, simply bask in the glow of the kind words as a way of developing your receiving muscles.

You may be suffering from a sense of indebtedness—the belief that givers and receivers keep a giant scorecard and are always checking it to make sure it's not lopsided. You may believe that if someone gets you a birthday present, you have to get him one, too—not because you want to give, but because you owe him. I know about this because I used to carry a giant scorecard around in my head with me at all times. Or, if you've ever told someone, "Let me buy lunch— you bought last time," then you know what it's like to keep score.

If you practice this kind of scorekeeping, then every gift you receive is also an obligation. If those obligations start piling up, you might never dig your way out. I used to discourage people from giving me gifts so that I wouldn't go into debt. Years ago I started inventing excuses about why we couldn't come to dinner when our friend Monica and her husband invited us over. She was an amazingly talented cook, famous for her handmade pastas stuffed with gourmet meats and cheeses and complex dinners fabricated with exotic Indian spices. I knew I wasn't ever going to be able to match Monica's culinary prowess. How could I have them to dinner, open a can of soup, and call it even? So after they'd had us over twice and we hadn't had them over at all, I started rejecting the invitations. Sadly, that was also the demise of the relationship, which fizzled a little later. Too bad I didn't know then that coming to dinner and enjoying myself would have been payment enough.

Gracious receiving means taking a gift just the way it's offered: with no strings attached. If you attach strings in the form of future commitments, you may feel more in control, knowing that you are keeping pace with the giver, but you will be unwittingly rejecting the very things you want more of in your life. Keeping score means limiting the things you can receive to what you can repay. Not getting even is allowing wonderful gifts, help, and compliments into your life without restriction. All you have to do is stop keeping a mental scorecard about who owes whom.

It wasn't easy for me to accept that idea when my friends gave John and me a weekend away for our anniversary. Part of me wanted to reciprocate by getting them grand presents for their special occasions, but I knew they didn't want to be repaid with a present of equal value in the future. It wasn't about equality for them. I didn't owe anything, so all that was left to do was have a great time and give a hearty thanks.

Feel Uncomfortable and Say "Thank You" Anyway

·······◦◦◦·······

Why should receiving gifts make us uncomfortable? Getting something material from someone else can make you feel awkward for a number of reasons. Maybe you worry that you don't have a reciprocal present, or that you don't really deserve what's being offered, or that you shouldn't need anything extra. Perhaps you'd prefer to avoid the spotlight you're under when someone has just given you something and is waiting expectantly for you to open it.

When receiving gifts makes you feel inadequate, immodest, or guilty, you have two choices. You can decide to react to your discomfort and reject the gift, or you can choose to receive it graciously even though you feel uncomfortable.

If you reject gifts because you feel uncomfortable, you'll keep yourself from having the things you want the most. If you find the courage to *override* your instincts to reject a gift or compliment and receive it graciously despite feeling vulnerable, you'll not only receive more of the things you want, you'll increase your tolerance for abundance, intimacy, and peace.

Being vulnerable enough to receive may always make you uncomfortable, but what you will be receiving will make you feel good—if you let it. You have to be able to stand both the discomfort and the goodness to be a good receiver.

Carrie was grateful to receive perfectly good baby clothes from a neighbor whose kids had outgrown them, but secretly she felt embarrassed about receiving them because she thought it made the family look needy. But if being able to use perfectly good clothes that someone else no longer has any use for makes you needy, then all of us are. By that logic, nobody should get a birthday present or a housewarming gift—unless they are somehow inadequate and don't have everything already. Each of us should be born already having everything we need—but, of course, we're not.

Carrie had also forgotten how good her neighbor felt about doing something nice for her, and what a pleasure it would be to see the tiny clothes on her baby. When the neighbor saw Carrie's baby wearing a jumper that her daughter had once worn, she cooed and asked to hold the baby. "This reminds me so much of when my daughter was little. Thanks for the memories!" she told Carrie, who felt a connection with the other mother as they both enjoyed the pleasure of feeling the baby's warmth beneath the pastel fabric. Clearly the neighbor received something, too—the wonderful memories of having a small child—and the joy of knowing that she was past the diaper phase!

This is the key: When you feel the temptation to reject a gift, remember that receiving makes the person giving the gift feel good, too.

It's not always easy to admit you're not completely together. Sometimes we want to be able to say we did everything ourselves. But since none of us can meet that requirement, you might as well let other people help you and contribute to making your life better.

When you've developed your receiving muscles and begin to receive graciously, everyone gets a gift. You also begin to develop the belief that you deserve good things.

Chapter 3

◦⟨⟩◦

SPEAK TENDERLY TO YOURSELF

Don't criticize yourself—ever. Harsh words make us both defensive and bruised, and our natural instinct to protect ourselves from criticism is to put up our guard.

You can't receive anything with your guard up.

Therefore, give yourself the same kindness and consideration you would bestow upon a good friend. When you're tempted to criticize or berate yourself, think instead of what you would say to someone you love and didn't want to hurt. Be as tender to yourself as you would be to her.

Make talking gently to yourself a discipline that you stick to no matter what. When you're receptive, you're open and light.

Don't fish for compliments by putting yourself down to see if others correct you. If you want to find out what people think of you or your work, ask them directly.

To love oneself is the beginning of a lifelong romance.

—OSCAR WILDE

GOOD RECEIVERS DON'T PUT THEMSELVES DOWN

I'VE PUT MYSELF DOWN in front of others as a way of protecting myself. I thought that if I announced my flaws or pointed out my deficiencies—before anyone else had the chance—I would be safe from criticism from others.

However, because I was already criticizing myself unnecessarily, I wasn't safe from *myself*. Hearing those harsh words come out of my own mouth was like taking a beating. No one else was likely to hit me as hard as I was hitting myself.

The sad part was that I was hyper-focused on faults that hadn't even come up.

For example, I made soup for some friends one time, and after watching to see if they liked it, I said to one of them, "You're having a hard time choking that down, I see." By giving in to my fear that the soup wasn't tasty, not only was I ungracious, I put us both in an awkward position. Instead of having the *choice* to bestow a compliment, he was *forced* to say something good about my soup in order to shore up my confidence. When he said, "No, no—it's very good," I accused him of lying to be polite.

The poor guy couldn't win at my dinner table. I'm sure I

was not much fun to be around that night. I was trying to be modest, but I actually put my friend in an awkward position and behaved ungraciously by calling him a liar. Instead of forming a pleasant connection with my friend, I had created an unnecessary conflict.

Putting yourself down is poor form to begin with, but then arguing with somebody who tries to say something kind about you on top of that adds insult to an already ugly situation. If you're wondering how someone is enjoying your soup, it's fair to communicate cleanly by asking, "How do you like the soup?" If the person says, "It's delicious!" then your job is to believe them and say "thank you."

My importance to the world is relatively small. On the other hand, my importance to myself is tremendous. I am all I have to work with, to play with, to suffer and to enjoy. It is not the eyes of others that I am wary of, but my own.

—NOËL COWARD

YOU'RE THE ENEMY INSIDE THE TENT

A FEW YEARS AGO my dad agreed to help me put new baseboards in our home. As we were working together on the project, I was startled to hear him cursing at himself from the next room. He would say things like, "Dammit, Peter! You're doing a sloppy job!"

27

I would try to reassure him that the baseboards looked fine—because they did—but he continued to scold himself. Nothing I said seemed to make any difference, which was irritating because I felt as though my opinion didn't count. It was also uncomfortable to see my dad so upset for what seemed like no reason at all. It was much ado about nothing, in my mind. Still, he was determined to yell at himself. Even when all the baseboards were installed, he was unrelentingly critical of his work. He marched around, touching the imperfections on the joints and muttering, "You should have made these smooth." I continued to tell him that I thought they looked beautiful and that I was grateful for the molding, but he didn't seem to absorb my appreciation for his help at all. He even winced when I was thanking him, as if it were painful to hear that I was appreciative and thought he had done a great job.

I'm familiar with that harsh voice—I have a similar one in my head. Hearing my father yell at himself made me more aware of my own tendency to do the same thing. I noticed, too, that the things I have said to myself are much harsher than what I would ever say to someone else. For instance, if someone else on my volleyball team tried—and failed—to pass the ball to the setter, I wouldn't say "You're playing is awful tonight—what the hell is wrong with you?" but I have said things like that to myself. To someone else I would probably say, "No worries—you'll get it next time."

Today, my rule is not to say anything to myself—even silently—that I wouldn't say to a friend. It sounds simple, but the implications of that rule are much greater than I first realized. For instance, since I would never say to a girlfriend, "I just hate your skin!" I won't say it to myself either. I wouldn't tell her that her house is a disaster, that she didn't work hard enough, or that she shouldn't have eaten so much, so I won't say such critical things to myself anymore either. If you can't picture yourself telling your best friend that she screwed up, don't say it to yourself either.

By saving yourself from harsh words, you are protecting your self-esteem and confidence. In short, you are making a commitment to yourself that you are going to feel good and not put yourself in the dumps.

A good receiver believes that she deserves wonderful things, but you won't feel deserving if you're speaking to yourself harshly. Instead, you'll feel the anxiety of being under attack, which will naturally result in feeling defensive. You can't receive anything when you've got your fists clenched and your dukes up. If you are in the habit of putting yourself down, you will instinctively reject other people's kind words when they come your way. Therefore, to be a good receiver, it's important to speak to yourself only with tenderness so that you can remain calm, centered, and open to the possibilities.

There's an old Persian saying that it's better to have one hundred enemies outside the tent than one inside. When you criticize yourself, you *are* the enemy inside the tent. Your defenses are always up because no place is safe. When you're defensive, you can't receive because you're busy trying to protect yourself. How can you be open and receptive when there's someone right inside your head yelling mean things at you?

You can't receive much of anything until you learn to talk to yourself with tenderness.

SOMETIMES SELF-CRITICISM IS SO FAMILIAR YOU DON'T EVEN NOTICE IT ANYMORE

OF COURSE, not all self-criticism is so obvious. Sometimes I judge myself harshly without realizing it. That's because that judgment lives so naturally inside my head that I don't question it.

In the past, I would refuse help when someone offered to clean up after a party at my house because I thought my kitchen was disorganized. I didn't want anyone to see that I had new shelf paper in some cabinets but the old ugly stuff in others and that some of my spices lived in the same drawer as the cheese grater, measuring spoons, and extra batteries. I was afraid someone would say to me, "Hey, why don't you organize your kitchen better. How can you be so lazy?"

Of course, none of my friends is likely to say that. I'm the only person critical enough to say something like that to me. This and other self-criticism lived so deeply in my head that I wasn't even aware of it. One night, after a friend offered to help clean up and I rejected her offer, I thought about why I had done so and realized that I was afraid of letting out the secret of my disorganized kitchen.

I didn't know I was criticizing myself, and hearing that in my head was costing me intimacy because it was preventing me from receiving. I was also making extra work for myself whenever people came over because I insisted on doing everything alone.

But I didn't know that at the time. I just knew I was afraid to let anyone else into my kitchen. It wasn't until I examined the *reasons* I was reluctant to receive in that area that I noticed there were harsh words in my head.

In that way, your reluctance to receive can be a clue about how you might be persecuting yourself unnecessarily. If you pull on that string by asking yourself why you just rejected something you say you want, you'll likely come up with an underlying self-criticism. For instance, if you feel squirmy inside when someone says you're a great mom, maybe it's because you tell yourself that you're not doing enough for your kids. That's a harsh criticism that you might not even realize you have for yourself until you see yourself struggling to accept a compliment.

That's how receiving (or not) can help you identify the critical things you say to yourself. And once you recognize them, you will see an area in which you deserve to receive.

The art of being yourself at your best is the art of unfolding your personality into the person you want to be. Be gentle with yourself, learn to love yourself, to forgive yourself, for only as we have the right attitude toward ourselves can we have the right attitude towards others.

—WILFRED PETERSON

A CRITICISM IS NEVER THE TRUTH

SOME WOMEN OBJECT when I encourage them to let go of self-criticism because they think that it's protecting them in some way. "If I don't tell myself the truth," they argue, "then who will?"

But criticism is NOT about telling yourself the truth. It's about judging. Maybe it's true that you have put on weight, but that's not the same as telling yourself you're a fat pig. See the difference? The truth is just the facts—criticism is attaching a cruel judgment to them.

You can be honest without being self-critical, but you can't be self-critical without getting defensive, and you can't be defensive and receptive at the same time.

Let's say my kitchen really is a deplorable mess and someone offers to help me wash dishes. I have two choices: I can either say no because I believe my kitchen reflects that I'm lazy, or I can say, "I'd love to have the help, but I'm too embarrassed to have you find out that I keep the coffee, dish towels, and shot glasses in the oven." *Now* I'm telling the truth but without berating myself. The friend who was offering to help has the chance to back away from the kitchen before anyone gets hurt, or she could say, "I don't care about that. Let's get these shot glasses clean and put them back in the oven." Now I get the warm feeling of intimacy from finding out that my friend loves me even if I'm organizationally challenged, I get liberation from my shelf-paper shame, and I get a clean kitchen in the morning—all because I refused to criticize myself.

Another option in this situation would be to acknowledge my self-criticism by saying out loud to my friend, "I can't let you near my kitchen because you'll see what a slob I am and you'll never want to eat here again." I would not only be criticizing myself, which is unattractive, I would put my friend in the awkward position of having to reassure me.

I suppose that the one good thing that would come out of it is that at least I would hear the self-criticism out loud and be able to address it directly. That's better than having it skulk around in my psyche while my conscious brain is unaware of it. With the harsh words out in the open, I stand a better chance of exiling them from my head. Once I hear them, I can assess them for truth and banish the judgment portion, like separating the wheat from the chaff.

Removing the judgments from your head—even if you didn't know you had them before—is going to help you feel safer. That's because none of us can really relax when we fear we might be judged, even if the judgment is coming from within us.

When my own self-judgments made me feel fearful, one of my coping techniques was to try to stay in control of everyone around me. For example, I would jump up to get whatever my guests needed during dinner to keep them out of the kitchen. That way, I figured I could avoid having other people notice the areas where I judged myself. Of course, having dinner at my house then wasn't terribly relaxing because I was always focused on keeping everyone out of the kitchen, not on listening to the conversation. It wasn't until I banished the judgments that I found the courage to relax without trying to change the subject or influence what others put their attention on. I felt safe in my own skin. From this relaxed position, I could receive help in the kitchen and let the conversation flow naturally—even if it included compliments for me.

When you stop criticizing yourself, you will relax and enjoy the people and world around you. The less you try to control, the more open you'll be to receiving the very things you say you want. Just as I would have enjoyed the comfort and laughter of good conversation if I had stopped berating myself about my kitchen, you will find something in your life that is lacking when you stop the negative tape in your head. You'll also be more relaxed when you know you're not going to be criticized internally. You'll be freer to invite others to see how you live, and you won't have to take yourself too seriously.

A big part of developing a tolerance for a better life is letting go of the familiar habit of beating yourself up with words. The sooner you stop, the sooner your guard will come down, and that is a critical part of attracting gifts, compliments, and help.

IF YOU CAN'T SAY SOMETHING NICE TO YOURSELF, FIND SOMEONE ELSE WHO WILL

IF YOU ARE FULL OF SELF-JUDGMENTS you won't feel deserving of tenderness or gifts. When you don't feel deserving, you can't receive what comes your way, so you unwittingly reject it.

What mean things do you tell yourself? If you berate yourself for not doing a good job at work, or for spending too much money, or for sometimes behaving like a bitch, try to get down to the truth of the matter.

The truth behind the criticism "You're not a good worker" might be that you don't put in as much overtime as your colleagues. The truth behind "You spend too much money" might be that you have debt because you used credit cards to survive hard times. The truth behind "You're a bitch" might be that you have more responsibilities than your nervous system can handle and so you're always overtired, and therefore you can't give your friends and family the time you wish you could.

Ask a friend you trust to help you identify the reality and separate it from the judgment. Once you have the truth, you can look at it objectively, instead of cringing with self-recrimination. Feeling like a bad worker will make you feel much more defensive than facing the fact that you work only forty hours a week while others at your company choose to work more. You might have the perspective that you have a more balanced life than the workaholics at your company. Now you can relax because you're no longer being judged.

Or let's say the truth behind your judgment that you're a

bad mother is that you work full time and are tired when you're with your kids. That doesn't make you a bad person, but it may be an indication of an area that you want to change. I'll talk more about that in the chapter on identifying your authentic desires, but for now work on separating the simple truth from your harsh judgment.

Stay open to gifts and speak tenderly to yourself, and you will begin to feel that you deserve good things.

Chapter 4

❧

PRETEND YOU'RE COMFORTABLE

No matter how uncomfortable you feel when someone offers you a compliment, gift, or help, if you act as if you are comfortable, you will soon begin to feel more at ease. The discomfort you feel when someone offers you something is in direct proportion to how deserving you feel of having it.

Have faith that there's plenty in the world for you by reminding yourself that affection, material objects, time, and energy can be replenished.

Be careful what you pretend to be because you are what you pretend to be.

—KURT VONNEGUT JR.

IF YOU ACT AS IF YOU DON'T DESERVE SOMETHING, EVERYONE ELSE WILL AGREE

LEARNING TO RECEIVE GRACIOUSLY will also make you more confident because it demonstrates your belief that you deserve happy surprises. If you reject gifts, compliments, and help—no matter how polite the reason—you send the message that you don't deserve those things.

When I spontaneously offered to help a friend of mine who is also a writer send out manuscripts, she first told me I couldn't because it was too much work. I suspect she didn't feel deserving of my help, because when I stood firm with my offer to review, print out, and mail her manuscript to a few contacts, she started listing all the steps I would have to take as though I didn't know what I was offering. "That would take up your time," she said, "and a lot of printer ink. And cost money for postage." Her voice reminded me of a mother trying to discourage a child from doing something foolhardy. "Are you sure you want to do this?" she asked sternly. Now my enthusiasm for helping her was turning to exhaustion. I did help her with her project, but she managed to take some of the fun out of it for me. Though I love my friend, she made me think twice about offering to help her again.

I think she felt guilty about imposing on me, even though I had offered to help. It was as though she weighed out what this gift would cost me and decided it was too much, which tells me she didn't think she deserved my help. Her belief went a long way toward persuading me along the same lines.

Abundance is, in large part, an attitude.

—SUE PATTON THOELE

THERE WAS NOT ENOUGH IN THE WORLD FOR ME

I USED TO SEE THE WORLD as a place where everything was in limited, dwindling supply. I formed this idea while watching my parents struggle to provide school clothes and sufficient attention to four kids. They were often caught short—so I alternated between only two pairs of pants in junior high and baby-sat for my younger siblings a lot. My scarcity mentality was reinforced as a young adult by my own commonly over-drawn checking account and too little energy remaining after a forty-hour workweek.

If there were so little of the basics in the world, how could I deserve special, frivolous things?

I believed that everyone had limited supplies that were further depleted when they shared. If you had four apples in your basket, I figured that giving one to me meant you would have only three—which made me feel as if I were denying you something. I didn't trust that you knew what you could spare—I imagined that you were overextending in some way and that I should take care of you. If I got by without the apple, I felt more virtuous because I was leaving more for you. But the apples that I refused because I felt guilty taking them sometimes spoiled while I went without.

I told myself I was taking the moral high road by not receiving because I believed if I accepted someone's apple, she would have to go without. But the world is an abundant place, and the more I take what's offered to me, the stronger and healthier I become, and the more I can contribute to a strong, healthy community. Others benefit when I'm thriving, so it's actually more considerate to receive what's offered to me.

However, I was raised to pull my own weight, and receiving seemed needy. If I got anything from someone else, I thought it meant I wasn't as organized or prepared or self-assured as I should be. To take from others made me feel deficient in that area. And being deficient, I thought, meant that I was undeserving.

I struggled with the feeling that I didn't deserve some of the gifts that came my way. If I were truly self-sufficient, I believed, I wouldn't need help moving, or those compliments, or that housewarming gift of a bottle of wine. Did my friends think I couldn't manage something as common as a move? That I was so insecure as to need constant compliments? That I wouldn't even have wine?

I also felt guilty when people spent money or time on me. At least with a compliment I knew they didn't have to expend a lot of effort or money to give it, but when something expensive or time-consuming came my way, I immediately thought about what the givers must have sacrificed for me. I would have rather had nothing than those feelings of guilt.

That's how I felt when some friends of ours offered to put up $3,000 so our band could record and press a CD. I cringed inwardly at the thought of accepting the money because I thought that if I wanted to make a CD, I should be able to afford it myself. But my friends didn't feel that way. They believed in me and enjoyed our music enough to finance the recording and pressing. Meanwhile, I felt undeserving of both the money and the compliment.

I took the money and made the CD, but I treated it like a debt that had to be repaid. Now, I can appreciate the wonderful gift I received from those friends, who still gather in my living room from time to time while we play the old songs from the days when I was in a band.

How to Feel Deserving

So WHAT SHOULD YOU DO if you're like I was and don't feel you deserve things that others offer you?

Simple: Act as if you do. If you pretend that you feel deserving, you'll become confident that you do.

If you transcend your own feelings of unworthiness by simply acting as if you feel comfortable when you're offered something, you will develop a tolerance for having the things you want most.

In the movie *Three Kings,* George Clooney explains the paradox of courage to a nervous army recruit who is afraid to take on a dangerous mission. He tells the recruit, "You just do the thing you're scared . . . to do, then get the courage for it afterwards."

That's how receiving works, too. If you receive a compliment, gift, or help that makes you feel self-conscious, you get the self-assurance of feeling you deserve it afterward. Therefore, deciding to receive graciously—whether you feel you deserve it or not—makes you confident.

Before Dahlia began a receiving regimen, she had a life full of aggravations: Her landlord imposed on her privacy. Dahlia single-handedly did all the housecleaning because she felt guilty asking her kids to help when they were so busy with schoolwork and gymnastics practice. She bristled every time someone complimented her artwork because she felt she could make each piece richer if she just had more time. Today, Dahlia and her family own their own home, the house is tidy because the kids pitch in, and her art is displayed in a gallery.

"Things improved for me when I learned to take help," Dahlia told me. "I got advice from a friend who had already bought her own home and knew the ropes, and from my brother, who introduced me to a gallery owner, and of course from my kids for the housework. I certainly feel more confident that life will continue to get better, and that my career as an artist will really blossom this year, because I know I don't have to do everything alone. Seeing my work in a gallery has made it easier to hear praise about it, because it's helped me believe that others might really like it. I no longer feel like they're patronizing me when they compliment me."

Sometimes receiving compliments makes us uncomfortable because it challenges our beliefs about ourselves. We're self-conscious when suddenly attention is called to an area in which we don't have confidence.

However, when you practice receiving, you expand your comfort zone and increase what you believe you deserve. That's what I mean when I say things will get as good as you can stand: If you can find the courage to receive things that you're not used to having, you'll start to realize that you do deserve those wonderful things. You'll build a tolerance for living better.

Faith is taking the first step even when you don't see the whole staircase.

MARTIN LUTHER KING JR.

RECEIVING REQUIRES FAITH

Of course, to do that you have to have faith.

The more you believe that there's plenty, the easier and more pleasurable it is to receive. At Thanksgiving feasts where the table is overflowing with food, we tend to fill our own plates and stomachs to capacity; we can see with our own eyes that there's enough for everyone. Receiving the things that are most important to us requires a little more faith because you can't always see the abundance around you. So, you must consider the offers that come your way as evidence that there's more than enough for you.

Tomorrow is going to be twenty-four hours long, so as long as you're alive, you're going to get more time. The same is true with energy. No matter how weary I get today, I can rest tonight and start tomorrow restored. If I run out of money, as I frequently do, I can earn some more. If I'm out of food, I can get more at the grocery store or grow some in my garden.

The point is that the universe is abundant because our most basic resources can all be replenished. The more you see the abundance in the world, the more comfortable you will feel receiving.

Once you're comfortable with taking a heaping portion of what's presented to you for your pleasure and enjoyment, you won't have to struggle or worry as much. You won't have the NET (needless emotional turmoil) or guilt when you receive the things that are offered to you because you won't be taking away from someone else's pleasure.

Chapter 5

GET OUT OF CONTROL

To receive, you must temporarily relinquish control. Underneath the urge to control is fear. Therefore, when you catch yourself rejecting or dismissing a compliment or gift, try to identify the underlying reason by asking yourself what are you afraid of. Ask yourself if your fear is realistic. If it is, what is the worst thing that could have happened if you had received graciously?

You might find yourself tempted to tell other people that they should also be receiving. You might offer to buy lunch and have someone say, "No, no—let me get it." With your new consciousness, you'll want to say, "Hey—receive, receive, receive!" But trying to control how someone else receives will only cause you to miss an opportunity to receive yourself. Focus on your own receiving instead.

The only thing that makes life possible is permanent, intolerable uncertainty: not knowing what comes next.

—URSULA LE GUIN

The best way to live is by not knowing what will happen to you at the end of the day.

—DONALD BARTHELME

RECEIVING MEANS FEELING EXPOSED

THE MORE WOMEN I MEET, the more I notice that most of us are far better at giving than receiving. We're quick to comment on a friend's gorgeous sandals or her delicious lasagna. We don't hesitate in deeming her ideas terrific or writing a card just because. But when the kindness is intended for us, we often insulate ourselves from it with comebacks like, "These are from last year," or "It's easier to make than it looks," or, the auto response, "You didn't have to do that."

One of the goals of the intimacy workshops I teach is for women to seek from others the connections that lead to intimacy (for more information about these workshops, visit www.superwomansolution.com). Because receiving graciously automatically connects the receiver and the giver, the first step is to make receiving a habit. I ask the women to participate in a receiving exercise by thinking of an authentic compliment for another woman in the class, such as "You have a beautiful smile" or "You are an amazing and supportive friend." Even though I've just reminded them to receive the compliment seriously and thankfully, many women make a joke or dismiss it. They say things like, "After six years of wearing braces, I better have a good smile," or "Saying I'm supportive makes me sound like a Jogbra."

These women always say the same thing—that it was easy to give a compliment but hard to receive one.

Why?

Because we feel in control when we're giving a compliment and out of control and exposed when we receive one.

When we're giving the compliment, we're focusing the attention away from ourselves and onto someone else. When we're receiving a compliment, we are aware that someone else has been observing us, which brings on a tsunami of self-consciousness. The next thing we know, our hearts are filled with vulnerability. That vulnerability arises from knowing that if someone can see our gifts, she can also see our flaws, and that if someone can make us feel good, she can also make us feel bad. We're exposed when we're receiving. If we weren't exposed, it wouldn't feel as meaningful—or as scary.

Human felicity is produced not so much by great pieces of good fortune that seldom happen as by little advantages that occur every day.

—BENJAMIN FRANKLIN

TO HAVE INTIMACY YOU MUST
GIVE UP CONTROL

············ഔ············

ACCEPTING COMPLIMENTS AND OTHER GIFTS often makes us uncomfortable because we are not in charge. Receiving is, by its very nature, passive. We don't ask for compliments, and so when they arrive, we may feel as if someone just made us appear immodest. Or we may fear that an unsolicited offer to help means that someone perceives us as weak.

My wanting to maintain a sense of control caused me to reject the things that women like to receive—compliments, apologies, help, gifts, and emotional support. I bucked up when I was overwhelmed instead of leaning on a friend, because I imagined that doing so would threaten my independence. I hid my sad feelings because I didn't want to be perceived as weak or emotional. I avoided people who would have gladly supported me when I felt vulnerable because I worried that they might see an Achilles heel and—who knows—use it against me some day, which, of course, was unlikely.

At the root of my discomfort when anyone gave me something before I became a good receiver was fear of being out of control. To receive, I *had* to give up control, if only for a moment, which fueled my fear by reminding me that life is unpredictable and won't always go according to my tidy plans. That meant I couldn't tell my friends and family not to spend a lot of money on me or to give me gifts only on my birthday. I couldn't be certain that they weren't sacrificing their own enjoyment for mine when they offered help. I couldn't ensure that they would give me something that I felt I deserved. Most frightening of all was the thought that their gifts could betray what I believed about myself, like when John said I looked beautiful that morning before my important meeting and I just felt stiff and frumpy in my old suit. Hearing something that contradicted my feelings about myself made me fear I was being patronized or mocked. I mistrusted his compliment—and therefore my husband—because I was so sure it wasn't true.

My desire to be in control was costly. It cost me the opportunity to receive compliments, gifts, help, and many other things I like. But the highest price I paid was in losing out on the emotional connections we gain when someone gives us something; intimacy is forged when we are pleasantly surprised—and flattered—by getting something we didn't expect.

In the old days, I passed up the opportunity to develop deeper relationships with just about everyone. I chipped away at the intimacy of my marriage every time I snubbed my husband's offer to take me out to dinner, protesting that we didn't have the time or money. I skipped a pleasant connection with the man at the dry cleaner because I rebuffed his offer to help me carry my bedspread out to my car. I passed up a chance to laugh and talk and to get to know my friend better when I rejected her offer to help me paint my kitchen. Naturally, the level of intimacy I missed out on varied depending on my relationship with the giver, but on lots of occasions I passed up a pleasant connection that would have made both my life and someone else's sweeter.

You might not think that it's so important to have a pleasant connection with the guy at the dry cleaner—and you're right, it's not going to drastically rock your world. However, it is important to your happiness and well-being to feel a part of the community, which is what happens when you receive from everyone in your community—even if it's just a neighborhood vendor.

We cannot adjust the winds, but we can adjust the sails.

—ANONYMOUS

DROP THE GUN AND PUT YOUR HANDS IN THE AIR

SINCE THERE IS NO WAY to stay in control and receive graciously, part of becoming a gracious receiver means surrendering control to people around you. It's a little like being on a ride at an amusement park; you can't steer, and you can't predict exactly what will happen next. But those are the things that make being on the ride so thrilling.

When I was writing *The Surrendered Single,* I learned that some single women want to be able to control who will ask them out. For example, Michelle couldn't resist calling a man who had taken her out the previous week because, she said, she was interested in seeing him again.

What Michelle really wanted, though, was to erase the vulnerable feeling she had in her stomach, which was caused by not knowing if or when the man she had dated—and liked—would ever call her again. She wanted to dictate when and where that second date would happen so she didn't have the uncertainty of wondering whether he liked her enough to call again.

In other words, she wanted to be in control.

True, being the first to call meant Michelle didn't have to wait for him and feel anxious about whether he would call. But Michelle's approach also prevented her from experiencing the thrill of hearing his voice on her answering machine if he called of his own accord. By staying in control, she was no longer in a position to receive his interest in her. What if her date hadn't called because he was waiting to secure reservations at a special inn?

That's just one example of how wanting to stay in control can keep you from getting wonderful gifts. Married women can be just as controlling and, therefore, ungracious. For instance, when Shelly's husband announced that he wanted to take her out to dinner, she said, "Are you crazy? We don't have time for a night out." Her response was not only impolite, it was downright hurtful. She missed the opportunity to receive his gift—an expression of love—and they were both worse off for the exchange. In one fell swoop she had rejected the chance to spend the evening alone with him and she had hurt the intimacy between them.

When you shut the door on the chance to receive a gift or dismiss one that is being offered, you are rejecting the gift giver and throwing away the chance for intimacy. If what you want is intimacy, then when the romantic lead in your life wants to give you something, receive it as best you can. To do otherwise is to reject it *and* him. Sure, Shelly got the ultimate say that night on whether they ate in or out, but that control cost Shelly something she says she wants more of: romantic evenings with her husband.

Even in friendship we often forget to receive graciously. For example, Tricia offered to pick up Jill's kids after school on the day that Jill was painting the kitchen, but Jill declined the offer by saying, "Oh, no—thanks. That's nice of you, but I'll just pick them up myself." Jill would have loved to have painted a little longer instead of stopping early to rinse out her brushes before driving over to the school. But she was also worried that Tricia would notice that her kids both had runny noses—again—and would think Jill was a bad mother. The only way to protect herself from being judged, Jill felt, was to refuse Tricia's offer. She stayed in control, avoided being vulnerable to Tricia's judgments (which were worse in Jill's mind than in her friend's), and, as a result, had to do more work and miss out on connecting with her friend.

A timid person is frightened before a danger, a coward during the time, and a courageous person afterward.

—JEAN PAUL RICHTER

RECEIVING IS TRICKIER THAN IT SOUNDS

STAYING IN CONTROL protects us from being criticized, disappointed, dropped, or otherwise broadsided. Receiving means we have to trust others even if we fear a compliment is meant to manipulate us, or that someone will criticize us for being arrogant, or that a gift will actually come with a price that we'll have to pay later. But why take those risks at all? Why make ourselves vulnerable?

Because we can receive only when we are willing to be exposed.

Receiving puts us in the spotlight for a moment, and in that moment we have a choice: We can be either open or defensive. When we're defensive, people sense that their efforts or compliments will be wasted—they know that we won't take them in, and they stop offering. Our body language and facial expression send out a signal that we don't need anything from anybody. A lack of vulnerability will come across as either arrogance ("I've got it all handled, so I don't need your help") or false modesty (contradicting a compliment we've just received). Either way, we're defended, which is the opposite of being vulnerable, and people know that nothing they give will get through, so they don't try.

Receiving—being open—takes courage. I have to let my guard down to accept something from someone else. That means I'm exposed—to both the greatest joy and the greatest pain.

Our instincts will tell us to avoid making ourselves vulnerable. That's why my modus operandi was to stay in control. What's more, I equated vulnerability with weakness, which is a terribly unattractive quality for an able-bodied and strong-minded woman to present to the world. Today, however, I no longer think of my vulnerability as repulsive; instead, I recognize that it's attractive.

We're afraid to be human because if we're human we might get hurt.

—MADELEINE L'ENGLE

STAY IN YOUR OWN SKIN

WHEN OTHER PEOPLE SAY they want to help, believe them. If they were just trying to be polite and they didn't really want to help, they'll learn a valuable lesson about speaking with their own truth when they watch you speak from yours.

For example, Fran's father was getting a new computer,

and he offered to give his old one to Fran's daughter, Ariana. But just as he was ready to pass the old one along, it died. Not wanting to go back on his promise to give Ariana a computer, he offered to buy a new one to give to his granddaughter. Fran was tempted to say, "You don't have to do that," but she remembered just in time that she was working on being a gracious receiver and so decided against it. Instead she said, "Thanks, Dad. That is so sweet of you. Thank you so much."

Later Fran told me, "I wondered if he may have felt obligated to get the computer for her. Of course we would have understood if he didn't give her one at all because the old one was broken. But I want to become a good receiver, and I really don't *know* what he was thinking. I didn't want to detract from his generosity by saying anything but 'thank you.' I'm minding my own business this time, and speaking for myself and for my daughter instead of trying to take care of him. If he was waiting for me to let him off the hook, I guess he'll learn for next time and offer only what he's comfortable giving."

Not trusting others to do what they want is like saying that you don't trust them to know themselves and make decisions accordingly. You are trying to jump out of your own skin and into theirs so you can decide what's best for them. You undermine their kindness and waste their strengths on petty arguments. That's just annoying.

It causes you to miss out on the pleasure of having whatever they were offering you and, moreover, the pleasant connection between the two of you.

> *As your faith is strengthened you will find that there is no longer the need to have a sense of control, that things will flow as they will, and that you will flow with them, to your great delight and benefit.*
>
> —EMMANUEL TENEY

I KNOW ONLY WHAT I WANT, SO I TRUST OTHERS TO SAY WHAT THEY WANT

I USED TO THINK OF RECEIVING as taking something *from* someone else. I couldn't accept Denise's help with the dishes because she had small children and was always cleaning up, and I didn't want her to feel that coming to my house meant more cleaning up. I said no to a coworker who offered me a ride to the mechanic to pick up my car because I knew she would be stuck in traffic if I accepted her offer. I urged my sister not to get me birthday presents when she was in college because I knew she couldn't afford them. No matter who was offering me something, I could always find some reason that I should refuse what was being given.

I told myself I was being thoughtful, but I was actually trying to control those people (and dozens more) because I thought I knew best how much they could afford to give. While I told myself I was being polite, I was actually distant, standoffish, and probably irritating to them; not only did I reject their offers, I was condescending. The message was that I knew better what was right for them than they did.

What made me think I knew what was best for them? Maybe Denise really needed the adult time she would have had talking with me while we cleaned up together. Perhaps my coworker knew that doing a favor for me would lift her out of her own problems. And why shouldn't I have allowed my sister the pleasure of seeing my delight in something she picked out for me in the same way that I love seeing her excitement when she opens something I've bought for her?

Since I can't read other people's minds, I had no way of knowing whether they were offering me gifts out of a sense of obligation or for the pleasure of giving. Treating their offers with skepticism was presumptuous and ungracious. Instead of trying to look at the situation from their point of view, I would have been better off—and seemed more con-genial—if I had looked at the situation from *my* point of view. Instead of saying to myself, "Should I let my colleague drive me to the mechanic even though she'll get stuck in traf-fic and be miserable?" I should have been saying to myself, "Do I want a ride to the mechanic?"

The question to ask myself if someone offers help with the dishes is not, "Does *she* really want to help or is *she* just trying to be polite?" but rather, "Would *I* rather do the dishes alone or spend the time with a friend who will lighten my load?" Then the answer seems clear. Of course, there may be times when the question is, "Would I rather have help with the dishes this evening, or should I do them myself in the morning, allowing me a chance to relax now?" If I decide to do them later, I would say *that*—not, "I'm sure you have to do plenty of dishes at home, so I won't make you do any more here." Telling someone how she feels is controlling and could very well make her defensive; no one likes to be controlled. That's not conducive to a close friendship, which can thrive only when you let others speak for themselves—and you believe them.

And believing others is necessary if I want to be a gracious receiver and let things get as good as I can stand.

Chapter 6

✧

RECEIVING COMPLIMENTS

To become more attractive, smile graciously when you receive a compliment, and thank the giver—even if you feel like a fake. If you fret, frown, or contradict the kind words, you'll appear ungracious.

Notice which of your girlfriends or female relatives are good receivers. Then think about which of them appear most attractive and confident to you. Look for the overlap.

We ask ourselves, Who am I to be brilliant, gorgeous, talented, fabulous? Actually, who are you not to be?

—MARIANNE WILLIAMSON

WHAT EVERY GREAT RECEIVER KNOWS

THE ONE SKILL a woman who wants to be confident and gracious must master is receiving compliments. It sounds rudimentary, but if you can't receive compliments, you won't be able to increase your tolerance for good things to come into your life. You'll inadvertently turn away the man who is perfect for you, refuse help that would make your life easier, and miss out on the intimacy you could have in your friendships.

Patty's experience illustrates this point beautifully. When she first became aware of the value of receiving, she noticed her tendency to refuse compliments about her looks. Whenever someone said, "You look great," she could think only of all the ways she wasn't quite put together. When a family friend, Geri, told her how pretty and summery she looked in her pink dress, Patty winced and covered her fingernails, which hadn't been manicured in a while. But the friend responded by making a face at her and said, "So what are you saying? That you're actually hideous and I just didn't notice? Fine—see if I ever give you a compliment again!"

Geri used a playful tone when she said those words, but

her message was clear. Finally, Patty recognized what she had been doing for years. She had been ungracious, had stung her friend with her rejection, and had even turned away future compliments. Right then, Patty decided to make a conscious effort to change. She resolved simply to say "thank you" to compliments about her appearance, no matter how uncomfortable she felt hearing them.

Not long afterward, Patty had lunch with an old friend, Jean, whom she hadn't seen for months; the last five times that they had made plans to get together, Jean had canceled at the last minute. During the lunch, Patty told Jean that she felt unimportant to her, that Jean's unwillingness to make their getting together a priority made Patty feel as though she didn't matter to her. Jean responded by saying, "I'm so sorry you thought that even for a minute. I love you and value your friendship so much. I would hate the thought of not having you as my best friend."

That's when Patty noticed something different. She told me, "Before I started practicing receiving, I would not have been able to take in those words fully. I would have dismissed them because it's uncomfortable to hear them. I get squirmy when people say such tender things to me. In the past I would have wanted to rush to the next part of the conversation, where I am not the topic. But instead I listened to my friend and really heard her words, and I understood that she had been under a lot of pressure at work, that our not getting together was about her work schedule, not her feelings for me. Listening to her made me feel wonderful and close to her. It also made me cry a little. I got to receive her love in a way I wouldn't have before."

Patty had worked only on the basics—receiving compliments. But the awareness and perspective she gained from exercising her receiving muscles led her to having a bigger capacity for receiving affection and having intimacy with a friend.

RECEIVING COMPLIMENTS WELL MAKES YOU MORE ATTRACTIVE

MY FRIEND'S MOTHER, Kim, made a gourmet lunch for her daughter's wedding shower. Everything was perfect—the buffet table looked like a photo spread from *Epicurean* magazine, and the meal was delicious. When I complimented her for a job well done, she looked happy and gave me an enthusiastic "Thank you!" She didn't apologize for anything about the meal or explain anything to me about its preparation. She just basked in my appreciation for that moment. Maybe she was thinking, I hope she didn't notice the poached salmon was cold, but I don't think so. I felt a small connection with Kim in that moment because I knew she had received my compliment. I could tell because she looked me in the eye when she smiled, which made *me* feel good because I knew I had made *her* feel good. The connection came from our mutual pleasure: my kind words made her feel appreciated, and her receiving them made me feel validated.

Later someone mentioned that Kim had also made the flower arrangements, and several people commented that they were gorgeous. Kim looked up from what she was doing in time to hear and receive the compliments on her arrangements; she gave us that easy smile and said "Thank you" again. By this time, I was thinking how beautiful my friend's mom is.

Finally, when the shower was over and all of the guests were getting ready to leave, I watched Kim as each of the women offered her praise for throwing a wonderful party. Not surprisingly, Kim took in each compliment. Again, she lit up with a beautiful, relaxed smile. She looked happy and confident hearing the praise.

Granted, Kim had done plenty that day that was worthy of praise, but the point is that she was able to hear that from us. Not everybody can. The more we praised her, the more radiant Kim looked, and the more contagious her smile was. She was enjoying the pleasure of hearing the compliments as much as we were enjoying the fruits of her labor. As a result of her response, I came away thinking of Kim as a warm, confident person, all because she had a great capacity for receiving compliments! I wanted to be as gracious as Kim because it was so attractive.

❋

Most of us have been raised to think that it's unattractive to bask in a compliment, but just the opposite is true. Imagine if instead of saying thanks when I complimented her on the meal, she had said, "It was nothing. I just copied recipes from a magazine." That wouldn't have been attractive at all. In fact, such a response would have seemed like false modesty, which is never attractive. I would probably have felt a slight irritation. Didn't Kim hear me? I would wonder. I might even have argued with her by saying, "It wasn't nothing! This meal required lots of preparation and care."

If Kim had done anything less than receive graciously, it would have reflected poorly on her. As it was, her graceful response to our compliments made her attractive and likable.

In order to be so gracious, Kim had to be willing to withstand the attention we were giving her, and to accept the compliments wholeheartedly and without apology. She was not in control of what we said or how we said it. Rather, she had to go with the flow in order to hear our praise.

Do not fear to be eccentric in opinion, for every opinion now accepted was once eccentric.

—BERTRAND RUSSELL

FEELING LIKE A FAKE IS BETTER THAN LOOKING LIKE A JERK

A MAN IN HIS SIXTIES once told a woman his age how beautiful she looked. She responded by saying, "Well, I'm not twenty-five anymore." Her response was not just ungracious—it was self-critical. The man was disappointed with her response on several counts.

"She didn't seem to have much self-esteem," he told me. "It made me sad that she didn't get any enjoyment out of being attractive. Even worse, her response left me feeling defensive. Did she think I would rather be with a twenty-five-year-old? I wouldn't. I just wanted to tell her how beautiful she was, but after she said that, she seemed less so."

I know it feels strange and uncomfortable to believe people when they're saying something that doesn't match what you believe about yourself. You feel vulnerable and anxious because you're afraid that you're going to be "found out." If someone says you're athletic and you think you're uncoordinated, you might feel nervous that the person with that image of you will learn what you think is the truth and deem you a fraud. Your instinct is to fess up before he uncovers the real you.

But if you reject him, you're rejecting the gift of his compliment and making yourself look like a jerk.

In the movie *Shallow Hal,* Jack Black is cast under a spell in which he sees people's inner beauty displayed as outer beauty; therefore, he sees the beautiful Gwyneth Paltrow when he looks at a three-hundred-pound woman who has a wonderful heart and sense of humor. When he tries to tell this woman that she's beautiful, she gets upset, tells him to grow up, and stomps off, even though she had been enjoying his company. Perhaps she was afraid that she was being set up for ridicule or some other cruelty. But Jack was just telling her the truth about what he saw—a beautiful girl. Not being able to accept that and getting upset made *her* seem like the jerk—not him. You could argue that she was just trying to be realistic, but she also could have enjoyed feeling beautiful and admired, since that was Jack's perception.

Isabel's situation was similar. She had a difficult time accepting compliments from her husband when she gained twenty pounds and it all went to her derriere. Fortunately, her husband loved her larger bottom, and he made up a rap song in praise of her butt. But all Isabel could think was, I have a fat butt! Instead of taking in her husband's compliments, she called him a liar and told him to shut up about it already. In her mind, it wasn't possible that her bigger butt was attractive to him, so she passed up a chance to feel admired and see herself through her husband's eyes. She was uncomfortable hearing words that contradicted her belief about herself.

If you insist on arguing with people when they compliment you, you, too, will miss out. That's why it's important to believe compliments—even if it makes you feel like a fake. You might still think someone who gives you such a compliment is just trying to be polite. That may be, or it may be that the soup you made *is* delicious.

Think you can stand that?

Chapter 7

⚜

TAKE ALL THE HELP YOU CAN GET

When someone offers you help, resist the temptation to delve into whether they really want—or can afford—to help. Instead, ask yourself if you want to receive what's being offered and respond accordingly. Some friends will help in small ways, and some may help in ways that seem too big to accept.

The more vulnerable you are when you ask for help, the stronger the emotional connection you will forge, and the greater the honor and compliment to the person whose help you are seeking.

We don't accomplish anything in this world alone . . . and whatever happens is the result of the whole tapestry of one's life and all the weavings of individual threads from one to another that creates something.

—Sandra Day O'Connor

Let Others Lighten Your Load

Receiving help can be hard. When someone assists us, we are, by our very actions, admitting that we need something—whether it's a ride, coaching, aid with a child, or simply placing a heavy bag into an overhead compartment. And needing help can make us feel weak or force us to confront our insecurities and imperfections. But receiving help is also the best way to give yourself more free time.

Getting help may make you feel inadequate because it brings into question whether you are capable of doing everything yourself. But since no one can do everything herself, that's not a reasonable question. The more important question is, How much are you willing to let others lighten your load?

Claire didn't understand the value of receiving help until she broke her arm when she was forty-two. "Strangers would offer to put my groceries in the car for me, and I would refuse because I still had one good arm and could do it myself," she told me. "Of course, it took me longer, but I didn't want to feel helpless. Then one day I was trying to put my luggage in the overhead compartment by myself and a man offered to do it for me. I told him I could do it, and I probably could have, but a woman nearly said, 'You have only one good arm. Let him help you for goodness's sakes!' That's when I realized I must have seemed ridiculous with one arm in a cast, saying, 'I can do it myself.' That's what two-year-olds say. What was I trying to prove?"

Claire told herself she didn't want to feel helpless and have others see her as helpless—or worse, needy—so she tried to stay in control by doing everything herself. That made her appear ungracious and slightly ridiculous.

"Now I realize that part of the reason I didn't want to accept any help is because I wanted to be able to feel superior to people who need help, but feeling superior is a lonely state," Claire admitted. "I'd prefer to take a little help now and then so I can be part of the community, even if it means I'm not better than other people."

As with rejecting gifts, rejecting help will also deny the helper the pleasure of knowing she's lightened your load.

There is great comfort and inspiration in the feeling of close human relationships and its bearing on our mutual fortunes—a powerful force, to overcome the "tough breaks" which are certain to come to most of us from time to time.

—WALT DISNEY

NO WOMAN IS AN ISLAND

YOU NEED HELP. Maybe you don't need psychoanalysis, but you do need the help of your friends, coworkers, children, and the occasional stranger. I know this because I need advice on how to handle my six-year-old nephew when he won't put on his shoes; I can't turn our mattress single-handedly; and the only thing that soothes me when I am overwhelmed is a pep talk.

I need help practically all the time.

All of us do.

Elly found this was especially true as she prepared for a three-day hospital stay for a hysterectomy. To be specific, she needed three teachers, several neighbors, her cousin, two families at church, her mother-in-law, and her best friend. And that was just for looking after her children. Everyone was happy to help, but Elly was ashamed that she needed it.

"It seems like I should be more together," she said. "Having to ask for help is like having to tell everyone that I can't do what I am supposed to do to manage the life that I chose for myself."

It's true that asking for help shows that you're not capable of doing everything yourself.

But who says you're supposed to conquer all of life's necessities single-handedly? Needing help doesn't make you pathetic or inadequate, but sometimes that's what we tell ourselves when we receive help.

Elly's large, enthusiastic support network was actually proof that she was well loved in her community—not that she was needy. Had she been a bottomless pit of need, it's unlikely that so many people would have offered to help her. Her circle of friends saw an opportunity to lighten the load for someone responsible who needed temporary support—not for a disastrous person who couldn't manage her responsibilities. Each of us is designed to be interdependent on others, and having surgery certainly makes us aware of that.

There's a beauty to that interdependence. In the movie *Witness*, the Amish community has an old-fashioned barn raising, where more than a hundred people work together to build a barn for a neighbor. They pitch in because they have already received help or will need help building their own barns, and because doing something for someone else is purposeful and satisfying. The barn-raising scene is quite moving; we see the power of the community taking care of its individuals and the vitality of the people who know they're doing something important for their neighbor.

The man who receives the barn at the end of the day doesn't apologize or feel pathetic because others helped him. There's no shame in not being able to build a barn all by yourself. He knows that he'll have his turn to contribute, and that his own success as a farmer will help make the whole community stronger.

The same is true for you: When you receive help, you gain something and you become stronger, and that in turn enables you to be a better citizen in your community.

No woman is an island. Receiving help reminds you and those who help you that you are part of a group that needs you just as much as you need it.

Trouble is a part of your life, and if you don't share it, you don't give the person that loves you enough chance to love you enough.

— DINAH SHORE

YOU HAVE TO BE VULNERABLE TO GET EMOTIONAL HELP

RECEIVING GOOD ADVICE or support will also make you stronger.

Your friends and family, colleagues and clients, and anyone else with whom you interact regularly have perspective that you don't—because they are not you.

Their input can help you out of a quagmire because they can see the proverbial forest through the trees. Therefore, a good receiver welcomes help and advice nondefensively and incorporates the wisdom and knowledge of the people whose lives touch hers.

To do this, she has to become vulnerable. And, that's the rub.

As a teenager more than twenty years ago, Yvonne had given up a daughter for adoption. Now in her thirties, she longed to make contact with her child, but she wasn't able to trace her because the records were sealed. She didn't want to ask for help with her mission because she didn't want to reveal what she considered to be a shameful past. Then she met Patricia—a stranger who sat next to her in a dentist's waiting room and explained that she was running late because she had been talking on the phone to the son she gave up for adoption twenty-two years earlier. Yvonne knew Patricia wouldn't judge her for her situation since she'd been there herself, so she decided to share her problem with the stranger—and to ask for help.

"I also gave up a child for adoption," Yvonne said haltingly, "and I would give anything to find her now. How did you do it?" Yvonne's eyes filled with tears as she asked the stranger for help.

Yvonne's honesty and vulnerability were an unspoken compliment that expressed, "I trust you to be gentle when I put down my armor. I feel safe with you." When you give someone such a gift, her instinct is to be tender so as to reassure you that she understands the honor. Vulnerability will draw people to you in a way that appearing invincible never could; others will identify with your humanity and be reassured by your authenticity. Even if Patricia hadn't shared the same experience as

Yvonne, Patricia would have responded to Yvonne with tenderness because that's what decent people do when you're vulnerable with them.

Patricia also felt complimented by Yvonne's question. The subtext of any request for such advice is, "I admire what you've done and I'd like to emulate you." Who wouldn't be flattered to know that someone wants to emulate her?

When Yvonne asked Patricia's advice, Yvonne put herself squarely in a position not only to receive the valuable information that eventually helped her contact her daughter, but also to receive support, validation, and an immediate connection with Patricia. Although she was nervous about revealing herself to a stranger, Yvonne was also relieved knowing that she was no longer alone with her secret, and she was especially grateful to have the number of a detective whose creative methods helped her discover her daughter's name and whereabouts.

Not surprisingly, Yvonne and Patricia became friends, and Patricia continued to support Yvonne through the process of reuniting with the daughter she hadn't seen in so many years.

Alone, all alone
Nobody, but nobody
Can make it out here alone.

—Maya Angelou

Rejecting Help Is Rejecting
an Emotional Connection

Receiving support from others is scary because to do so we must make ourselves vulnerable. We're revealing our weakness, and our instincts tell us not to.

My best friend, Cathy, for example, was wonderful at being vulnerable; she would even call me in tears when she needed comfort and support. I was happy to give it, of course, because I naturally felt honored and connected to her at those times. But I was in the habit of wiping my own tears, so I never called her until well after I was calm and collected.

One day, Cathy confronted me with the inequality in our relationship and said that the imbalance made her uncomfortable. Because I never gave her the opportunity to comfort me, she felt that she was missing out on the opportunity to offer me a gift. Cathy wasn't keeping score so much as she was looking for a deeper connection with me than I was offering. I realized that if we were going to have quid pro quo, I was going to have to let my guard down even further with her.

I didn't want to fall apart in front of anyone. I much preferred being the woman who offered assistance—not the one who needed it. In other words, I didn't want to show a soft underbelly. However, if I maintained my "everything is always right with me" facade and didn't open up to Cathy, I was going to lose the closeness with her that can come only from an equitable friendship. Our emotional connection, vital to our intimacy, was on the line. So I resolved to be vulnerable with her, even though part of me resisted.

Shortly after we had that conversation I read a critic's harsh review of my first book, which hurt like crazy. I knew that Cathy wanted to give me the gift of her shoulder to cry on, so I forced myself to call her. As soon as I heard her soft, patient voice, I started sobbing, while she stood by quietly on the other end and soothed me. My whole body relaxed because I knew I was safe and loved even if I wasn't finishing my sentences or making any sense. It felt wonderful to have her tenderness, and it took our friendship to a new level. I couldn't have received that gift without a little humility—I had to admit that I needed help.

I quit therapy because my analyst was trying to help me behind my back.

—RICHARD LEWIS

GET ADVICE FROM PEOPLE WHO HAVE WHAT YOU WANT

THE FIRST TIME my friend Rachel made a cheesecake, its consistency was too soft. It looked more like pudding than cake, but she served it to her dinner guests anyway. One of them asked, "What makes cheesecake firm anyway?" Rachel made everyone laugh when she replied, "How should I know?"

Obviously, Rachel wasn't a great source for expert advice on making cheesecake that night, and she knew it. (Her humor, by the way, was a wonderful alternative to self-criticism.) If you were really looking for tips on how to make the perfect cheesecake, therefore, you'd have to look elsewhere; you can get good advice only from people who have already done what you want to do.

In my seminar How to Attract and Marry the Man Who's Right for You, I encourage women to find a married mentor who has the kind of marriage they hope to have someday. I advise them to call this mentor when they have questions about their dating lives, and to refrain from soliciting advice from their single girlfriends who don't have satisfying relationships.

One of the single women in my seminar took issue with this idea. "My friends call me for advice about dating, and I think I give great advice," she argued. Perhaps she *was* giving her friends good advice on how to form and nurture an intimate relationship. More likely, however, she was suggesting they do the same things that had kept her single. All she knew about dating was what she had experienced herself. A single woman doesn't know how to advise you on the path to attracting a great relationship any more than someone who lives paycheck to paycheck knows how to advise you on putting money away for retirement.

A friend who always looks put together can give you great tips on what to wear, but you wouldn't ask someone whose houseplants are brown for gardening tips. Your corporately employed friends can't advise you on how to start a business, and your out-of-shape friends can't help you get buns of steel. While they might have seen something about it on an infomercial, they simply don't have the experience of doing it.

A good receiver is quick to ask for advice, but she is also careful to ask an expert: someone who has demonstrated know-how in that area. This criteria is especially important when it comes to choosing a therapist, yet I frequently hear about women paying someone who's divorced to give them relationship pointers or having weekly appointments with a guy who's overweight to be hypnotized for weight loss. I can understand how that happens. When you're in a lot of pain and someone tells you he has the answers that will stop the pain, it's tempting to believe him—even when the evidence suggests otherwise. However, paying someone for advice when he simply doesn't know how to solve your problem can make the problem far worse. Therefore, be very picky about from whom you take advice. Regardless of whether you're paying him, ask your would-be mentor specific questions to determine if he has what you want. And remember, actions really do speak louder than words.

"Help one another" is part of the religion of our sisterhood.
— LOUISA MAY ALCOTT

TAKE MY ADVICE—I WON'T BE NEEDING IT

I F YOU SEEK OUT AN EXPERT in an area you want to improve and you tell her that you admire what she's accomplished, you are giving her a huge compliment. Doing so, even if you don't realize it, creates a connection to that person. People are flattered when you ask for their expertise, and if you actually follow their advice, you give them an even greater tribute.

Naturally, you have to decide if the advice fits before you follow it. A good receiver stays in the moment, doesn't get defensive, and considers what someone she respects and admires tells her. That can be a challenge if what your expert suggests seems disagreeable or absurd to you. Your knee-jerk reaction may be to ignore it, but a good receiver is willing to try something different at least for a little while.

That was my instinct years ago when I asked a woman the

secret to her long, happy marriage, and she told me that she tried never to criticize her husband, no matter how much he seemed to deserve it. I had an unhappy marriage at the time, but I thought her advice was ridiculous and old-fashioned. To me, refraining from criticizing my husband was dishonest. I also secretly believed that unless I told him what he was doing wrong, he would never improve.

I listened politely to the woman with a marriage I admired, but I decided I would not follow her advice. Although she had been willing to share her best tips with me, I simply wasn't willing to receive them.

Of course, that meant I still had the frustration and pain of an unhappy marriage. The misery didn't abate, and eventually I was motivated to reconsider her advice. She had planted a seed, and ultimately I reasoned that my constant criticism of my husband might just be what was hurting the intimacy in our marriage.

I decided that I would try—just as an experiment—to refrain from saying anything critical to him. That's when I discovered I wasn't able to stop criticizing him—at least not at first. My habit of nit-picking and complaining about him was so ingrained that I couldn't shut it off right away.

Maybe the real reason I didn't like the advice was that I didn't want to have to change.

Over time I finally did break my bad habit, and I did just as the wise woman suggested. And you know what? She was right: My marriage improved as if by magic.

Your ego may tell you to resist advice that would never have occurred to you, but it's worth repeating: A good receiver is willing to try something different at least for a little while. Most decisions are pretty easy to reverse if you don't like the results. If refraining from criticizing my husband didn't make my marriage more enjoyable, I could always start up criticizing again.

Being willing to endure the discomfort of the unfamiliar is part of developing a tolerance for better things.

Chapter 8

✣

BE STILL AND KNOW THAT
YOU ARE NOT GOD

Be still. Let other people do things for themselves as much as possible. Consider giving less to others and doing less for them.

Make a daily to-do list for the purpose of getting it out of your head. After you write it, look to see if there's anything on it that you can delegate to someone else—or at least ask for help with. Make lists of who could help you with a given project.

Once you've delegated everything you possibly can, go through your list again and ask yourself if everything has to be done today. If not, put it off until tomorrow, or at least make it a low priority.

You will no longer be the busy superwoman you once were.

What a relief.

> *Besides the noble art of getting things done, there is the noble art of leaving things undone. The wisdom of life consists in the elimination of nonessentials.*
>
> —LIN YUTANG

THE CURE FOR THE CHRONICALLY BUSY

ACTIVITY CAN BE ADDICTING.

Jumping from one task to the next can give you a high, and checking things off your list leaves you with a sense of accomplishment. When I let someone else help me, I sometimes feel nervous about not doing my work myself because I'm running the risk that there won't be anything left for me to do. That means I won't get the high of knowing I did a million things in a day.

But doing something all the time doesn't make you a better mother, wife, worker, or friend. It doesn't make you happier or more lovable. It doesn't even make you more productive.

It just makes you busy.

There's nothing wrong with being busy, but if you're *always* busy, it could be that you're choosing efficiency over intimacy. That means you're rejecting the very thing you say you want—more help and support, and the closeness that naturally results from taking help.

That was the case for Danielle, whose grown daughter asked her one night while she was visiting if there was anything she could do to help clean up after dinner. Danielle said, "No, everything's done," so her daughter went off to read. Then Danielle picked up a broom and swept every inch of the large kitchen—alone. She felt that she could sweep better and faster than anyone else. In rejecting the help, she embraced her desire to control. And she rejected her daughter in a small way, too. Her sweeping up by herself signaled to her daughter that Danielle felt her daughter wasn't capable of helping successfully; instead of cleaning up together—perhaps talking and thinking about the fun they would have the next day—they went their separate ways in the house.

The opportunity for intimacy was lost.

The most difficult thing in the world is to know how to do a thing and to watch someone else doing it wrong, without commenting.

—T. H. White

Should You Get involved?

If you identify with Danielle, maybe you've needed to work very hard to survive, or maybe you were raised with a strict work ethic, or maybe you feel guilty when you're not doing something. You might think that no one does as good a job as you do, which might be true; in that case, you need to ask yourself how important perfection is. Perhaps you have so much responsibility you don't feel as if you can rest for a second. Maybe you believe, as I once did, that you would have a lot more free time if life were less demanding. I remember thinking that if only I didn't have so much to do, I would be able to relax more.

In fact, I had to relax *first* to realize I had less to do than I thought.

Sometimes we give up the chance to relax by jumping in to take over someone else's job. Elise told me the story of how she decided to have a housecleaner come in, but she would feel embarrassed if her house wasn't clean already when the woman got there. She explained that she hated so much for the cleaning lady to see what a mess her house was that she cleaned everything before the hired help arrived—as though a houseguest were coming. Since Elise was doing all the cleaning herself anyway, she decided she didn't want to keep paying the woman for her services, so she stopped. Instead of letting the housecleaner ease her responsibilities, Elise made the whole experience even more stressful by doing the woman's work for her before she arrived.

Talk about not being good at receiving help!

The worst thing about this ridiculous story is that Elise said several other women in her neighborhood did the same thing. Naturally, none of them found relief from their responsibilities this way because they didn't let the hired help do the job. What a waste!

You might be tempted to jump in and help your coworker do a report that you know you could do faster or better. Sometimes it's tough to tell where your responsibilities end and someone else's begin, or whether it's important to help someone else with her responsibilities.

When you're not quite sure, you can ask yourself these questions to determine whether or not you should get involved.

Q. **What am I afraid will happen if I don't help this person?**

A. *I'm afraid that my coworker is going to do a poor job.*

Q. **Is my fear realistic?**

A. *Yes. My coworker is in the middle of a messy divorce, and I know she's not focused right now. Therefore, I'd say my fear is realistic.*

Q. **What's the worst thing that can happen if I don't help with the report or do it myself?**

A. *We won't get the new business, and things will be slow next quarter. If profits are low, the company may need to downsize and my job could be in jeopardy.*

Q. **Is it worth it for me to spend my time and energy on this?**

A. *I don't want to lose my job, so yes—it's worth my spending time to make this report optimal.*

Or consider the same scenario with a slightly different weightiness:

Q. **What am I afraid will happen if I don't help this person?**

A. *I'm afraid that my coworker is going to do a poor job.*

Q. Is my fear realistic?

A. *Probably not. She may take a lot longer to do it than I would, but in the end, it's just a quarterly report—nothing really critical.*

Q. What's the worst thing that can happen if I don't help this person or do the report myself?

A. *It probably won't be as well organized. Others may not grasp it as well as I would like.*

Q. Is it worth it for me to spend my time and energy on this?

A. *Not really. I can save my energy for something else.*

In the first example, it makes sense that you would spend your time, energy, and concentration on the report because the outcome really does impact something important to you: your job. In the latter example, however, you can feel the temptation to take something over and then decide that it's not necessary to invest your time because nothing critical is hanging in the balance.

Once you can make that distinction, you'll be well on your way to being able to relax and enjoy an easier life.

<hr>

My theory on housework is, if the item doesn't multiply, smell, catch on fire, or block the refrigerator door, let it be. No one cares. Why should you?

—Erma Bombeck

<hr>

The Danger of Doing Everything Yourself

I F YOU'RE VERY BUSY all the time, it could be that you have a lot of responsibilities—many women do. However, if you're busy doing things for other people, then it could be that you spend a lot of your energy giving. It's nice to give, but it's even better to receive—especially if you're frazzled and overwhelmed with all that you have to do.

If you're a mother who does a lot for her children, you might read this and think, But I have to do things for my children because they're not capable of doing things themselves. It's true that small children need constant help, but as they get older they are capable of doing things for themselves. I know a six-year-old boy who makes his own bed and prepares his own lunch to take to school. I also know a teenager who does the family grocery shopping (from a list) now that she has her own driver's license. So if you have a lot of responsibilities in your family, look around and see who might be capable of contributing more—and proud to do so.

Make the following your mantra: Don't do for others things that they're capable of doing for themselves. Obviously, a six-year-old can't drive himself to school, so you'll still have to do that. But he can make a peanut-butter-and-jelly sandwich all by himself.

If you're not sure what another can do for himself, the best way to find out is to leave him with a challenge and see if he rises to it. Give a child the task of making his own lunch for school and see how he does. Ask an employee to spearhead a project and then make yourself available to help as necessary. Let your teenager plan a menu and cook dinner for the family (but be prepared to order a pizza).

As a mother, it can be scary to let your child use a sharp knife, cook with hot oil, or even plug in a vacuum cleaner for the first time. However, if you don't help your child to stretch and increase her capabilities, you create a dependency that leaves you doing all the work. Let her do what she can and you unburden yourself while helping her learn self-sufficiency. Since grown-ups are just big kids, the same rules apply with the adults in your life. It bears repeating: If they can do it themselves, let them.

Work is the greatest thing in the world, so we should always save some of it for tomorrow.

—Don Herold

You're Not the Fire Department

I T'S EVEN OKAY TO DO NOTHING when your husband or son asks you to iron his shirt at the last minute before an important meeting. In fact, it's a good practice to say no to things that will make you resentful later. Even if you know you're capable of ironing the shirt in a hurry and doing a great job, better to say no than to feel put out because it made you late to yoga, or even if it only made you have to drive fast to get to yoga.

You might worry that someone else's school or work is more important than your yoga class, which is just a leisure-time activity, but before you go down that road, remember that if you are exhausted and depleted, you'll be no good to anyone—not even yourself. You certainly won't be in good receiving posture.

One way to help yourself make wise decisions about when to volunteer to help and when to decline is to say, "Let me think about it and get back to you." I absolutely love this phrase for giving me the luxury to think about my response to a number of situations where I'm unsure how to proceed. I always have a better response when I've thought things through. Be wary of helping out in situations when there is no time to think about what's best for you. Emergencies seem very exciting and urgent in the moment, but sometimes they turn out to be nothing more than someone else's bad planning that causes you NET (needless emotional turmoil). Plus, my experience is that responding to emergencies just begets more emergencies. If my husband knows that I will bail him out by producing a clean shirt at the last minute, he may unconsciously come to expect me to do that time and again.

You may feel guilty for saying no to such a request, but my friend Lynn lives by this rule: "I'd rather feel guilty than resentful." When she has to choose between doing something that will make her resentful or *not* doing it and feeling guilty, she chooses the guilt. "I find that people are pretty understanding when you have to say no, so the discomfort is over quickly. But if I do something I'm resentful about later—that could last for days and harm the relationship."

In my experience, feelings of guilt never last as long as a festering resentment.

The trouble with life in the fast lane is that you get to the other end in a awful hurry.

—JOHN JENSEN

GIVE UP THE RUSH

SOMETIMES YOU'LL GET AN OFFER that sounds nice but threatens to take too long. I've rejected a friend's lunch invitation because I thought meeting her at a restaurant would eat up too much of the afternoon. And I've waved away help in the kitchen because I figured I could get dinner on the table faster if I chopped the onions myself.

But when I say no to offers like these it usually has more to do with my unwillingness to break my habit of rushing around than really being unable to spare the time.

So what if I linger over sushi and don't run every errand on my list during lunch? Socializing over a meal will calm and center me in a way that makes me realize I have more time than I think. If I'm bent out of shape when dinner is delayed an extra five minutes because my husband or a friend doesn't chop as fast as I do, then I probably desperately need to relax in those five minutes anyway.

Years ago I was in that very situation—making dinner with my husband, who was cutting up vegetables and telling me a story. I wasn't hearing a word of the story because I was waiting for the vegetables to get cut so I could put them in with the chicken. Every time he'd stop cutting to emphasize a point, I'd focus on how he was messing up the timing of the meal. I wanted to say, "Please finish cutting those so I can listen to the story," but I wanted neither to interrupt to let him know I wasn't listening anyway, nor to criticize his pace. I was so focused on the task in front of us that I missed any chance to laugh and engage with him, to let the story transport me out of my harried, impatient mood. Instead of having fun while we were working together, I made the work drudgery for myself. We weren't going anywhere that evening, so what was I worried about?

Earlier in the day I had been rushing around trying to finish my work; by dinnertime I still had a leftover sense of urgency. I didn't know how to change gears. Staying focused on finishing tasks in a certain time frame instead of simply receiving the help caused me to miss the delights right in front of me—like the aroma of dinner and the pleasure of being with a man who tells me stories while he chops vegetables.

Maria felt the same impatience in the kitchen when her children were helping her, but she says her motivation for wanting things to move quickly is from exhaustion. "I just want the work to be over so I can rest," she explains. "But at some point if I'm not patient with the kids and don't let them make things themselves, I will end up still having to fry their eggs when they're eighteen years old, and that's not good for anybody."

Not receiving help—even if it takes longer—can be a trap that keeps you having to do everything.

> *Never confuse motion with action.*
>
> —ERNEST HEMINGWAY

SOMETIMES LESS REALLY IS MORE

ON THE DAY OF HER DAUGHTER'S high-school graduation, Janine left the house with what seemed like an impossible to-do list. Instead of planning a strategy for getting done everything she needed, she and her daughter headed out armed only with their faith that everything would work out.

They meandered through town and stopped at a tea shop for mango iced tea. From there, they dropped in at the hair salon, where a stylist was able to take the daughter right away, even without an appointment. Next, the pair decided to browse at a department store, where they found Father's Day cards and gifts, end-of-the-year presents for teachers, a skirt, the perfect bra, and decorations for the graduation party they were throwing the next day. Janine was amazed that by taking such a relaxed approach they finished all the errands by noon and had time to eat a leisurely lunch.

"I think you have to be relaxed to find that kind of serendipity," Janine told me. "It wouldn't have worked out that well if I had planned it and rushed from place to place."

While Janine wasn't receiving help from anyone in particular, she approached the day with confidence that she would find everything she needed without killing herself. They were receiving peace and a great time together instead of feeling stressful and anxious that things wouldn't get done. In other words, she was trusting that her relaxed approach would yield the things on her list. And so it did.

Focusing on trying to cross everything off your list can not only make your chores more difficult to complete, it can make you miserable. You make yourself a slave to the list and end up having a harder time completing it as a result. In my experience, serendipity prefers the company of a receptive woman to a woman who is rigidly driven to complete the tasks at hand.

There's a lot to learn from wasting time.

—NEIL YOUNG

BUSY ISN'T BETTER

I USED TO BE BUSY ALL THE TIME, which made me feel as if I was getting a lot done. The problem came when I noticed that being busy didn't ever end—there was always more to do. Looking back, I think being busy had a lot to do with wanting to feel as if I was earning my keep. And it's not just me—a lot of Americans are raised with that old Protestant work ethic, with the notion that idle hands are the devil's playground. That's part of our cultural baggage.

I was afraid that if I wasn't doing something it meant I was lazy. I worried that other people would see me that way, too, especially if my house needed to be dusted, my car needed to be waxed, or my garden needed to be weeded. Everyone could see those things, and I figured they were wondering why I didn't get to work. The only valid reason for not doing those things, I thought, was if I was busily rushing off to do something else—like working late or running an errand. That meant there was never time simply to do nothing, which was just as well because it helped me avoid my feelings that I was undeserving of living well.

The result of becoming a conscious receiver has been that I rest and play more and work less. I'm definitely not as busy as I used to be. I have plenty of downtime. I know how to be *still* now. Ironically, I'm just as productive and accomplished as I ever was, even more so—but I'm far less stressed out and less tired. I've come to see that busy isn't better—it's just busier.

I've come to value doing nothing; it gives me time to reflect on what's important, so I'm making choices that lead me to the best life possible.

Chapter 9

⋄

FILL YOUR OWN CUP FIRST

Spend time and energy making yourself happy every day.

Do at least three things a day for your own enjoyment, such as taking a nap, having lunch with a friend, meditating, taking a walk, or doing a crossword puzzle. This will not only make you feel well taken care of, you'll feel more grounded, too, which will make it easier for you to keep your balance when difficulties arise.

Others will be drawn to your poise and be more likely to offer you gifts, help, and compliments because they'll recognize that you'll neither drain them with neediness nor refuse their offers.

All of the animals except man know that the principal business of life is to enjoy it.

—ANONYMOUS

RECEIVING REQUIRES A FULL CUP

WHEN YOU DON'T TAKE TIME for your own pleasure, you run the risk of becoming drained, which leads to feeling needy. Neediness is a sure way to block yourself from receiving from others, who will recognize the hallmarks of a bottomless pit and steer clear. You can't control what your husband, boyfriend, boss, kids, or staff will do, but you can control your own energy reserves by taking good care of yourself. Others will be more willing to help you if you are already content than they will if you're running on empty and are about to drain them of everything they have.

Unless you fill yourself up by making sure you get enough rest, play, nutrition, pleasure, socializing, hugs, solitude, and affection every day, you're going to begin to feel needy.

Needy is not the same as receptive. In fact, they're opposites.

When you're receptive, you're already fulfilled. That means you're not desperate for anything because your basic needs are met. You've given yourself eight hours of sleep, spent time socializing, read something stimulating, grounded yourself spiritually, and moved your arms and legs to get your blood pumping. Life is not perfect, of course, but you're content, and then somebody comes along and delights you further by inviting you out to the movies (you accept), sending you home with the leftover gazpacho after a dinner party (you gladly take it), or commenting that your new haircut looks fabulous (you say "thanks"). When you're receptive, you're pleased to have the niceties that are offered, but you don't "need" them the way you need water when you're dehydrated and stranded in the desert.

When you're needy, on the other hand, it's because one of your most basic requirements—food, sleep, love, fun, solitude—hasn't been tended to. When that happens, it's easy to lose perspective and feel that someone else could or should be making you feel better. Neediness is the mistaken idea that if someone else would just do what you want him to do, you would feel relief from your misery. A good example is feeling lonely and thinking that if only the man you see at your coffee shop would ask you out on a date, you would feel better. Another one is being overtired and feeling that if only your family members would pick up after themselves, you could get more rest. If you haven't had any fun for a while, you might reason that your boss is working you too hard and wish that she would just lighten up.

But the truth is, none of those problems can be solved from the outside. The only cure for loneliness is to call or see the people who already love you, even if none of them is Mr. Right. The only cure for being overtired is to rest. And the only cure for being overworked is to take a break from working. And guess what? Only you can make any of those things happen. That's the thing about neediness—the cure is always an inside job.

Naturally there are times when you actually *need* help—like a ride to the doctor for a blood test, or some extra chairs for Thanksgiving. Those things don't make you needy—just human. They aren't problems only you can solve—they are simple, one-time things that friends will gladly help you with if they can—and if you don't approach them from a place of neediness.

Jennifer recognized this difference when one of her friends, Georgia, was always complaining about her medical problems. No matter what Jennifer suggested, Georgia said it wouldn't work and went right on complaining about how much pain she was in. Jennifer found herself inventing reasons to reject Georgia's invitations to spend time together because she was tired of the complaining. But when her friend Barbara came down with the flu, Jennifer was quick to drop by with some chicken soup and medicine from the drugstore.

"I felt like I wanted to do something nice for Barbara when she was sick even though she probably wasn't suffering as much as Georgia does," Jennifer said. "But I felt like I could brighten her day, whereas with Georgia I don't think anything I could do would make her feel better. Stopping at Barbara's felt light and easy and even made me feel good afterward. With Georgia, I have a hard time getting motivated even to talk to her, much less go over there with soup."

By tending to her own self-care, Georgia probably would have felt less desperate for someone to listen to her complaints, which in turn would have made Jennifer more inclined to want to help. To borrow from Ben Franklin's famous maxim, Friends help those who help themselves.

No One Can Fix Me but Me

W HEN I'M FEELING NEEDY (and all of us do, from time to time), I generally want my husband, friends, parents, siblings, work associates, or anyone else in sight to fix me, but I'm just setting myself up for disappointment by looking in all the wrong places for relief. Once I'm back in balance after I've focused on my self-care, I naturally attract more of the things I felt desperate to get when I was needy: spontaneous affection, compliments, attention.

The difference between being receptive and feeling needy is that receptivity is light. If you get something, you think it's great. You're pleasantly surprised that someone is doing you a good turn. You would have been fine if you hadn't gotten anything. You feel good already.

Neediness feels miserable because you're unhappy and usually self-pitying. It's caused when you have let yourself get too

- Hungry
- Exhausted
- Overwhelmed
- Overworked
- Lonely
- Frustrated

Being in any of these states will contribute to a loss of perspective. When you're experiencing neediness, it's because you're depleted of something, and there is no material gift, thoughtful compliment, heartfelt apology, or helping hand that can quell it because it wasn't caused by anything outside of you. Rather, neediness is the result of having been inattentive to your own requirements.

One of the hallmarks of neediness is when little things set you off. Your son left the milk out on the counter; instead of realizing he simply forgot, you wonder why he is doing this to you. None of your friends calls you to make plans for the weekend; instead of figuring they're busy with other things, you feel abandoned and left out. Your roommate, boyfriend, or husband fails to take out the garbage again; instead of brushing it off, you go ballistic. Why? Because you have no reserves left. Your cup is empty.

How to Lose Friends and Irritate People

WHEN NEEDINESS SETS IN, you unwittingly broadcast it to everyone who comes in contact with you by wearing a dejected or cranky look on your face, snapping at people, and sighing in frustration. One sure sign that neediness is coming on is the delusion that you'd be happy if only someone else around you would change. Another is that you're complaining—again. A third is a sense of urgency that your problem be addressed *now*.

In fact, neediness is the beginning of a vicious cycle that compounds itself because it alienates the people around you—the very ones that you fantasize could make you feel better if only they would do what you want. Instead, people naturally recoil from desperation. When you're needy, people around you pick up on it and realize that no matter what they do for you, it's not going to be enough. So they stop trying to do anything for you because they sense that their efforts won't make a dent.

The way to break the cycle is to avoid the depletion that leads to neediness. In other words, you have to practice good self-care.

Leah was relieved that she wasn't available to talk on the phone when her friend Suzanne called and said, "I really need to talk to someone right now." That's because Leah suspected that her friend was calling with yet another litany of complaints about how Suzanne's husband didn't pay enough attention to her. Something about Suzanne's tone and her urgency told Leah this conversation was going to be just as miserable and draining as the last few on the same topic. Early on, Leah had tried making suggestions and consoling her friend, but nothing seemed to help the situation—or put an end to the complaining.

"It seems like he's interested in me only if I'm making other plans," Suzanne had said previously. Leah imagined that Suzanne's husband, Josh, was probably just as eager to avoid being around someone who was clearly a bottomless pit of need.

The next time Leah spoke to her friend, she gently told Suzanne, "I know you're in a lot of pain about your marriage right now, but quite honestly I can't listen to your complaints about Josh anymore; it's draining me. I don't see any improvement in the situation, and I would just prefer we talked about other things. I'm sorry, but I just can't hear about that topic anymore."

Suzanne was clearly hurt and angry, and initially she reacted with even *more* neediness. "I don't have anyone else to talk to about my problems," she told Leah. "I thought you were my friend."

But a few days later Suzanne called Leah with a new tone.

"I think you did me a favor by telling me you couldn't listen to my complaints anymore," she started. "At first, I was just mad at you and felt you weren't there for me. But then I noticed that Josh is reacting to me the same way, but not being as direct. I figured he was avoiding me because I was so unhappy. So I made an effort to have a really great weekend whether he was paying attention to me or not. I got plenty of rest, went for a bike ride on the beach, took myself to the movies, and read a Dave Barry book. I was giggling while I was reading when Josh came up behind me and put his arms around me. My first instinct was to say, 'It's about time you paid attention to me!'—but I didn't. Instead we laughed together, talked, and enjoyed the evening."

This time, Leah was happy to listen—not just because Suzanne had solved her problem, but because she no longer sounded urgent, desperate, and miserable.

Clearly, Suzanne's neediness was driving away both her

husband and her friend. Fortunately, she discovered a way out of the neediness trap. The key for Suzanne—and the rest of us—was tending to her own needs. Only then could she receive affection from her husband as well as support from her friend.

It really is nearly impossible to keep perspective when you're depleted. Recently I went to bed too late the day before I was traveling across the country. When my flight was delayed, which caused me to miss my connecting plane and made my day even longer, I was really cranky about it. You'd have thought from my reaction that I was being forced to *walk* across the country. I wanted the airlines to fix my problem, but there was only so much they could do. Even if they *could* have done something more for me, I bet my needy approach wouldn't have inspired them to do much of anything but try to get rid of me.

The bigger problem was that I had no perspective because I lacked sleep—something only I can give myself. I tried to improve my attitude by telling myself I was just overtired, but that went only so far. It wasn't until I got a good night's rest that I regained my sense of well-being and became receptive—instead of needy—again.

The time which we have at our disposal every day is elastic; the passions that we feel expand it, those that we inspire contract it; and habit fills up what remains.

—MARCEL PROUST

SELF-CARE IS A DISCIPLINE

THE BEST RECEIVERS are people who know how to make themselves happy and relaxed. They do this by deliberately doing things they enjoy every day. They beautify their home, go to the gym, make something with their own two hands, or watch a sitcom for no reason other than because it makes them feel happy. They do these things as part of their routine—just the way you make your bed or brush your teeth—because it keeps them grounded. The discipline of self-care is just as important as keeping your home tidy or preventing plaque buildup. It helps you guard against depletion and build a tolerance for even more pleasure and enjoyment to come into your life.

Women who practice self-care have enough reserves to handle the unexpected challenges that life throws at them. The fringe benefit is that they emanate a sense of calmness and happiness that makes them enjoyable to be around. They have an undeniable aura of self-respect.

It may not always be convenient to fit enjoyable activities into your day, but good receivers do it anyway because they have faith that they'll feel better and more grounded when they do. I've had to force myself to go play volleyball in the evening when I was tempted to work longer, but I'm always glad afterward. The change of scenery and pace gives me a more positive perspective. I am now one of those women I used to envy, the one who has a lot of fun rather than the bedraggled one who wishes she were having fun.

Consider doing at least three things a day for your own pleasure. For instance, you might go to a yoga class, read the funnies, and make out with your boyfriend. The next day might find you sharing your lunch hour with a friend, reading a magazine, and getting a pedicure. You could play with your child or a pet, spend half an hour gardening, and soak in the tub. Going to bed early, having a sensual meal, getting a massage, singing or playing an instrument, listening to music, taking a class you enjoy, and meditating are also excellent examples of good self-care.

Your list of daily pleasures will probably include some of these things, but you'll also want to add to it those activities that are uniquely enjoyable for you.

Be picky about making your self-care something you enjoy—not something that someone else would like. For instance, when a coworker offered Vicky theater tickets on a night when she had a tennis lesson, she was clear that she couldn't go because she was much more excited about the tennis lesson than the show. For Vicky, going to the theater was only okay—whereas playing tennis was a joy. Sure, she would have enjoyed the show, too, but sticking to her original plan was better self-care.

Sometimes you'll schedule your self-care and something will pop up to interfere. Remember, though, that the crafts class, coffee klatch, or solitude you were planning is just as important to a gracious receiver as the other tasks on her to-do list.

A well-spent day brings happy sleep.

—LEONARDO DA VINCI

FORMING A HAPPY HABIT

IF YOU'RE LIKE MOST modern women, you're busy and don't have several extra hours in your day for self-care. That's why the most important step in practicing good self-care is planning it. Otherwise, it just doesn't happen. Work really will expand to fill the time, unless you make an effort to carve out the time you need to go to the beach or take a nap.

If I plan my self-care and then commit to a friend who will hold me accountable, that's even better. For some reason, knowing that my best friend will chide me later if I ignore my self-care gives me extra motivation to work it into my schedule, plus we supply each other with inspiration and ideas. Call it the buddy system—studies show it works to keep people exercising, and I find it works for staying on a self-care regime, too. I've been preaching the benefits of self-care for five years now, and to this day, I still talk to my best friend on the phone most mornings and commit to three things I will do for my enjoyment.

Practicing good self-care makes me more productive. Maybe that's because it keeps me from getting depleted, which in turn makes me feel more energized and capable. It's easier for me to finish my work or straighten the house when I'm feeling strong and motivated.

Now that I'm in the habit of making myself happy every day, I can't imagine my life any other way. I feel so much more grateful and fortunate because I live so richly. My friendships are stronger, and I'm much more clear about how to honor my needs. I rarely feel sorry for myself because I never get anything or do anything. Instead, it seems as if I'm always going to a game or a party, seeing friends, or relaxing. The result is that I'm much more receptive because my cup is already full. I can always use more compliments, help, or presents, but I'm not looking for them, or anything else, to fix me.

Tending to my self-care was a big change in the way I treated myself. Years ago, I ran myself ragged, complained bitterly about being overwhelmed, then collapsed in a heap at the end of most days. I thought things would get better some-day in the future, although I didn't know when. I even found some perverse pleasure in not indulging myself in things I loved because I felt more virtuous knowing that I wasn't do-ing anything frivolous. Unfortunately, I was also cranky and hard to live with because I was so short-tempered. I was con-stantly trying to control my husband because I was afraid that I was going to have to pay more, wait longer, or have more to clean; I knew I just didn't have the reserves to handle any such problems. I also felt unappreciated for all my sacrificing— which nobody asked me to do—and never felt as if I was get-ting as much as I was giving. I wished someone else would take care of me, but instead I acted like a porcupine by prick-ing everyone around me with my crankiness. I was always stressed out, always angry. I was unwittingly sending out a message to everyone near me that said, "I don't want or appreciate simple pleasures, so don't waste your time giving them to me."

Not so anymore. Now that I spend more time and energy on things I enjoy, others see that I'm someone who deserves to be enjoying herself. In other words, I'm setting an example for how they should treat me by the way I'm treating myself. It sounds so simple, but I never recognized before that others respond to me the same way I respond to myself, which was pretty much like Cinderella before she went to the ball.

Practicing good self-care is like deciding to be the princess who lives happily ever after.

Chapter 10

❋

OWN YOUR GIFTS

You have talents that bring value and enjoyment to you and others. If you don't know what they are, or if you are afraid to acknowledge them because you fear you'll seem immodest, you'll deny yourself the wonderful feelings of self-confidence.

Instead of trying to downplay your beauty or abilities, acknowledge that you have gifts that others admire and envy. Start by acknowledging your talents privately. Go in the bathroom, close the door, and look yourself in the eye. List the things you admire about yourself out loud. Take a thorough inventory of your gifts: Are you an incredible cook, a great listener, a savvy businesswoman? Be truthful with yourself. Be grateful for those attributes. Say, "I'm glad I have curly, thick black hair" or "I love being so articulate."

When you adopt an attitude of self-respect, others will treat you the same way you treat yourself. Conversely, putting yourself down in front of other people by waving away their compliments will be contagious: others will value you less, too. People see you in the light that you present, so if you are always putting yourself down by saying things such as "I'm fat," "I'll probably never get married," or "I'm such a klutz," you'll present yourself poorly.

Your perception of yourself will influence how others see you, and they will reflect that view back to you; that perception will become a reality.

If there is a single quality that is shared by all great men, it is vanity. But I mean by "vanity" only that they appreciate their own worth.

—YUSEF KARSH

MODESTY IS DISHONESTY

W HAT DID WE ALL LEARN in junior high school? Don't act like you're "so great." If you do, people will think you're stuck up and no one will want to befriend you. It's no surprise, then, that as grown women we've internalized that juvenile mantra and we strive for modesty. Our favorite means to humility is to contradict people who compliment us so that we won't appear arrogant. You like what I'm wearing? It's old. You think I'm attractive? Thank God for makeup.

Arrogance is unappealing, but so is false modesty. It's annoying—not endearing—when you tell someone what a great job she's done decorating her home and she says, "Actually, it's a mess right now." What does that say about you? That you like pigpens? That you don't know elegance when you see it? Suddenly, the person giving the compliment is undermined, and the person for whom it was meant has dismissed it so quickly that she hasn't enjoyed the praise at all.

Hyper-modesty can frustrate the person who's trying to give you something. You might be tempted to contradict a compliment for the sake of appearing humble, but when you do, you rebuff—and hurt—the giver, and that's an ungrateful—and unattractive—way to respond to kindness.

Although the melody is beautiful, I've always winced at these words from "Amazing Grace"—"how sweet the sound That saved a wretch like me"—because of the word *wretch*. I'm no beauty queen, but God gave me pretty eyes. I'm no genius, but God made me smart. I'm no comedian, but God gave me a sense of humor. Denying that I'm pretty, smart, or funny is not modest—it's a lie. If I can't appreciate my own gifts, I might as well not have them, yet our culture is full of suggestions—like the one in "Amazing Grace"—that we should actually put ourselves down to be more spiritual or likable. Naturally, no one wants to appear arrogant, but calling yourself a wretch is just as unattractive.

Humility means you acknowledge your gifts, but you keep them in perspective.

Modesty says, "I have two left feet," when really you're graceful and rhythmic.

Arrogance says, "I'm the best dancer there ever was."

Humility simply says, "I'm a great dancer."

If you can't acknowledge that you have a talent for dance when you do, it's like having a fabulous car that you can't drive. Modesty keeps us from enjoying the gifts we've already received and hampers our ability to take in new ones.

Stephanie had a gorgeous voice, but when some of us asked her to sing at a party, she shook her head. "I'm out of practice," she protested. "You don't want to hear me sing." But we already knew she had a wonderful voice, so we persisted in our request. "C'mon, Steph, just one song!" we clamored. She insisted that she wasn't going to sound that good, at which point I started to feel irritated. We were complimenting her, and she was contradicting us. What's more, her reasons for declining to sing were inauthentic. Instead of connecting with her while she sang, we were twisted up in a silly conversation of yes-no, no-yes.

I know that Stephanie didn't mean to sound so artificial; I suspect she was trying to appear modest. She was probably trying to be polite in a way that many of us were told to be polite—by knocking our own talents.

Or, maybe Stephanie was feeling insecure or nervous—that can happen to anyone—but she didn't say that. Instead she tried to claim that she wasn't a good singer, which just isn't true; her words were a boomerang to our kindness. If she had said, "I'm feeling a little shy," or even, "I don't want to right now," that would have been understandable. We might still have tried to cajole her to perform for us, but we would not have doubted her sincerity.

Every child is an artist. The problem is how to remain an artist after growing up.

—PABLO PICASSO

IT'S HARD TO BE HUMBLE

LOTS OF WOMEN I meet have a hard time acknowledging their gifts. I ask the women in my workshops to participate in an exercise in which they announce their best physical feature to the woman next to them. I ask them to look another woman in the eye and to fill in the blank in the sentence, "I have a gorgeous ———." Some women have a terrible time with this, even though they have many gorgeous features. In fact, I'm amazed at how often someone will try to say she has a great personality or a strong back just so she doesn't have to single out an attractive body part. Oddly enough, it's often the *most* physically attractive women who have the hardest time with this.

A woman in Atlanta who was struggling to say she had anything gorgeous said, "I don't think it's attractive to brag about yourself this way." I agreed that bragging was not attractive, but I pointed out that we were doing the exercise to practice enjoying our strengths—just among ourselves— since denying them was equally unattractive. I asked her again to tell us what she had that was gorgeous, but she looked down and said that most of her features were un-attractive and that those features stood out the most.

The whole group wailed in protest. Another woman turned to her and said, "We all have problems with the way we look, but that doesn't mean we can't appreciate at least some parts of ourselves. Just focus on those." Finally, after much encouragement, we learned that this woman felt she had gorgeous skin. And it was true—she did. There was nothing unattractive about her declaration—it was endearing because we saw her find the courage to claim what was right-fully hers even though it made her feel vulnerable to put her-self in the spotlight. Seeing her grasp the good feeling of enjoying her own beauty—even for a fleeting moment—was satisfying and inspiring.

But it did seem a shame that she had never been able to bask in the pleasure of being blessed with gorgeous skin before that moment. Maybe someone had criticized her for enjoying her skin in the past, and so she had learned to avoid acknowledging that she had anything worthwhile for fear of being knocked down. A lot of us have had that experience, but that doesn't mean we have to let it permanently keep us from celebrating ourselves.

Granted, it can be nerve-racking to be in the spotlight with our gifts or talents. It's not unusual to squirm when we feel everyone else is focused on us. We might be tempted to discount our abilities just to relieve the pressure of feeling as if everyone is looking at us, but when we do, we tell a lie and frustrate those around us who know the truth.

A good receiver knows what she's got and is not afraid to admit it. She's grateful and honest about her talents, which makes her all the more enjoyable to be around.

Chapter 11

⟨✴⟩

IDENTIFY YOUR AUTHENTIC DESIRES

Sometimes we don't even know what we want. When that happens, take a step back and ask yourself, "What is it that I really want?" This is the indispensable first step toward receiving what you wish for.

Instead of dismissing your desires as whims, trust and value them. Figure out what you want—big or small, impossible or realistic—even if you feel uncomfortable. The more you're willing to listen to your desires, the more they'll guide you toward getting what you want. This will help you know what kinds of help you want to receive.

Assess your desires daily. Even the truest desire can change unexpectedly. It's perfectly fine to change your mind. What you want now may be very different from what you want next year, in the spring, or after lunch.

> *The things that one most wants to do are the things that are probably most worth doing.*
>
> —Winifred Holtby

Only Dead People Don't Want Anything

Maybe you want new shoes, a nap, a break, a baby, or a chance to be in the movies. Some women crave a mansion, solitude, a garden, a husband, or eyelid surgery. Your desires may include a stiff drink, a better job, a great book, more savings, or a new friend. Whatever it is you want is an important part of who you are and who you're becoming.

I remember my parents telling me to be grateful for what I had, as if that would put an end to my wanting. Gratitude is important, but no matter how grateful and pleased you are with what you have now, it doesn't prevent you from wanting something else. For example, if you have a baby and you want another one, it doesn't mean you aren't grateful and thrilled to have your oldest—just that you have the capacity and the longing to receive another addition to your family. The same is true with material things—you can be happy you have a gorgeous dining room set and still lust after the new flatware you saw in a store window. There's nothing wrong with that. Wanting beautiful flatware means that you are a person who likes beautiful things. Denying your desires is denying a part of yourself.

Pure desire is very different from having a sense of entitlement, which is the expectation that you are owed something or have a right to something. Entitlement is ungracious, unattractive, and presumptuous, but it's not the same as desire, which is free of expectations. Wanting to go to the theater five nights in a row means that you have an appetite for culture—that's just you, and there's nothing wrong with you. However, going into debt to have those tickets would be irresponsible and would reflect a sense of entitlement. See the difference?

Your desires don't make you needy or demanding—just human. And being human pretty much guarantees that you will always want *something*.

That doesn't mean you're doomed to a life of discontentment—just that your desires will grow and change with you.

The great question—which I have not been able to answer—is, "What does a woman want?"

—SIGMUND FREUD

WILL MY REAL DESIRE PLEASE STAND UP?

OF COURSE, not all desires stem from a healthy place. Sometimes we know we need *something*, but we miss the mark. We go for a doughnut when we really need a good cry. A new pair of shoes takes the place of feeling someone has listened to us. A glass of wine makes us feel relaxed when what we really need is to work less. Acting on those kinds of desires can lead to disasters like having more clothes than will go in the closet and not being able to fit into any of them.

It's human nature to look for a superficial fix when you're not clear about what your real desire is. Fortunately, it's easy to tell the difference between an authentic desire and a fix because the latter will always be accompanied by a sense of urgency.

I can tell that I'm off track with my desires when I get into what I call the spin cycle. That's when I spin around and around trying to figure out a way to get what I want—*right now before it's too late.* Too late for what, I don't know. I just know that I want what I want urgently. Of course, getting that fix is never satisfying because I haven't addressed the real desire.

So how can you honor your desires without gaining weight and abusing your credit cards? The trick is to delay the urge for a fix and think of the urgency as a cue to dig deeper. For instance, could you wait until tomorrow to buy that outfit, or does it have to be right now? If it feels like it has to be right now, it's a good time to call a friend or stop shopping long enough to journal for five minutes. If you don't want to spend even a few minutes journaling before you eat that candy bar or drink that glass of wine, chances are it's not what you're really craving. Once you realize you're feeling urgency, you also have a clue that there's something you want that you haven't identified yet. Make an effort to find out what that is, and the urgency diminishes. It's much easier to resist the fix.

Ironically, if you don't mind delaying getting something you want, there's probably no harm in getting it.

Knowing your desires well is another way to avoid settling for fixes instead of the genuine article that you desire. Spend some time contemplating what you want. If you meditate on the question "What do I want?" on a regular basis, you'll have an easier time separating out the true desires from the fixes.

Meditating doesn't have to mean sitting cross-legged and chanting—it could mean folding the laundry in silence, or going for a long walk alone. Ask yourself, "What is it I really want?" To have some solitude? To get some advice? To set limits with my kids? To tell my boss I can't work late? I sometimes ask myself, "What will make me feel good?" The answers often vary from a big bowl of fruit to a Devil Dog to a nap to time to get my work done to help with a project that feels weighty.

A much more important authentic desire will always reveal itself when you stop the spin cycle and reflect inwardly. Once you know what you desire and begin to honor it, nothing can stop you.

It's a helluva start, being able to recognize what makes you happy.

—LUCILLE BALL

DON'T BE AFRAID OF IMPOSSIBLE DESIRES

OFTEN WE RESIST acknowledging what we want because we're afraid that we won't get it.

For instance, once when I was teaching a workshop, I asked a woman if she wanted to reconcile with her estranged husband.

"I don't know if he wants to," she answered.

I asked her again, "I understand, but what do you want?" She just looked blank. "Would you like to be reconciled with your husband?"

"I'm not sure that's possible," she told me.

"If it were possible," I persisted, "is that what you would want?"

"I don't know. Maybe," she finally admitted.

I suspect that she *did* want to reconcile, or else why would she be at a workshop to help wives regain intimacy in their marriage? But she was convinced that her husband did not want to reconcile, so she didn't even allow herself to have her *own* desire, and I understand this: she was protecting herself from disappointment and rejection.

She did not want to be vulnerable.

Perhaps conveying her pure desire to reunite would have caused her husband to respond to her differently. Maybe just looking him in the eyes and saying, "I miss you and I want you back," would have been enough to make him want to try again. After all, expressing a tender desire also reveals a vulnerability that leads people to want to help you.

All receiving requires that you have the courage to take at least some risk.

Surely reconciling her marriage would have been more important to her than indulging her fear that she would experience the pain of rejection if she expressed a true desire.

As Ambrose Redmoon wrote, "Courage is not the absence of fear, but the decision that something else is more important."

We are guilty of giving you too little because we are desperately afraid that you don't really want any more.

— DON BRESNAHAN

DESIRES ARE NOT DANGEROUS

PERHAPS YOU'RE THINKING you have to keep a tight rein on your desires or they'll get you into trouble. For instance, you might consider your desire to go to the beach on a workday something you'd best keep in check. But don't forget the reason you have the job is because it provides you with something else you desire—a salary and financial stability. What you have now are conflicting desires—one that says drop everything and feel the sand squishing between your toes and one that says let's be certain we can pay the rent next month.

So honoring your desire means that you first acknowledge it, and then let it guide you. Maybe your desire to go to the beach would lead you to take a day off and play in the waves or to plan a vacation with plenty of beach time. It could mean that you begin cutting back your hours or looking for a different job that affords you more time for the beach.

Or maybe your desire has more to do with ditching work that isn't a good fit for you, in which case it's an important signal that you should consider looking for a new job. You don't have to know what it is—you just have to be willing to admit that the job you have now isn't it by saying, "I want a job that's more fun" or "I want to change careers."

In other words, what your desires are whispering to you may actually be the key to something bigger than a day at the beach.

> When you jump for joy, beware that no one moves the
> ground from beneath your feet.
>
> —STANISLAW J. LEC

WHEN YOUR BRAIN AND YOUR HEART ARGUE,
YOUR HEART ALWAYS WINS

WHILE DESIRES THEMSELVES are not dangerous, ignoring
them can be. Trying to squelch them not only wastes your
time and energy, it can be downright embarrassing to admit
that you were less than authentic when your truth comes
out—as it almost always will.

Margaret and her husband were both high-powered exec-
utives when they conceived their first child. Margaret realized that the maternity-leave program where she worked was
terrible, and she fought to make a company-wide change that
would afford her more flexibility after the baby came. Other
women in the company were grateful for the sweeping
changes she instigated; however, Margaret herself never got
to enjoy the spoils of her victory because as soon as the baby
was born, she turned to her husband and said, "I'm never
going back to work."

That was sixteen years ago, and she never did.

Margaret was mortified to have to share this news with
her employer, who was understandably upset by this sudden
change of plans after she had implemented the leave program

that Margaret wanted. Margaret could have avoided the embarrassment if she had acknowledged what she had felt nearly nine months before the birth of her baby: that she wanted to be a stay-at-home mom.

"I realize now that I knew it then," Margaret says, "but I tried to talk myself out of it, to tell myself to be logical. But seeing my baby's face made it impossible to ignore my heart."

Karen had a similar experience. She had convinced herself that she didn't want to get married. She even made a list of a hundred reasons not to get married, which she enumerated on dates. She did this because she thought that guys liked women who were independent, and that this would remove their fears about whether she was trying to trap them into getting married. So instead of a true desire, Karen was saying what she thought men wanted to hear; as a result, no one proposed marriage or even wanted to date her for very long.

Finally, a married woman told her that it was okay to want to be married. Karen could no longer ignore her own truth—that she very much wanted to be married to the right man. That made all the difference. Shortly thereafter, she met Kevin, started a wonderful romance, and was happily engaged within seven months.

See how powerful it is to honor your true desires?

Some luck lies in not getting what you thought you wanted but getting what you have, which once you have got it you may be smart enough to see is what you would have wanted had you known.

—GARRISON KEILLOR

DESIRES ARE ROAD MAPS TO DESTINY

DESIRES ARE LIKE an inner compass that points the way to the next important step for you—whatever that is. For instance, in my twenties, I worked in an office, but I wanted to be a singer. Every day my desire would poke and prod me to do something about getting me out of my cubicle and onto a stage. So I took action, starting with singing lessons. Next I wrote song lyrics and asked my husband, John (who was already an accomplished musician), to put them to music. John and I put together a band and booked gigs to open for bigger bands.

At first I was self-conscious and nervous, but the more time I spent on stage, the more confident I grew. We recorded a CD and promoted it ourselves. I even persuaded the *Los Angeles Times* to write a review, and we started selling our music in legitimate record stores like Virgin and Tower. I accomplished all of this because my desire to be a performer propelled me. None of it would have happened if I hadn't acknowledged that desire. Recognizing what I wanted was the first step to getting it. Granted, it was a small step, but it was also an indispensable one.

Then one day the band broke up, and my hopes of becoming a singer were dashed. Sure, I could have started up another group, but I was tired. For a long time I had been spending all my energy on rehearsing and promoting, and all my spare money for flyers, photos, and microphones. I was disappointed that we never got to do that world tour I had imagined, and I felt all my efforts had been in vain.

I was also sad because I no longer felt passionate about being in a rock band. I wasn't as thrilled to perform as I had been at first. The momentum of our group had carried us for months after my desire—once so strong—had waned. I had moved on without realizing it, and that meant I didn't have the comfort of a challenge and a goal to work toward. Where I once had a passion for something, there was now a vacancy. It was time for a change.

Two years later, I decided to write my first book, *The Surrendered Wife*. Once again, my desire was strong and motivating. I drew on the writing classes I'd taken in college and typed it on a five-year-old home computer. John helped me publish the book, and, drawing from our experience with making and selling a CD, we promoted it ourselves. Again, I persuaded the *Los Angeles Times* to write an article about it, and we started selling the book on our website and through Amazon.com and Barnes & Noble.

Because of our experience with self-publishing a music CD, we knew what to do to promote my book. In just a few months we successfully sold out the first printing of the book, a feat that attracted the attention of a top-notch literary agent. Through his efforts, Simon & Schuster agreed to publish *The Surrendered Wife,* and it became a bestseller and generated letters of gratitude from women all over the world.

In retrospect, I could see that all my hard work with the band was not in vain. What seemed like a total bust was actually important preparation for a future accomplishment. My time on a stage with a rock band had given me the confidence I needed to talk about my book on TV. If I hadn't had the desire to sing, or hadn't acknowledged it, I wouldn't have been ready when it was time to promote my book. I don't know of a class or training program that could have prepared me as well. Simply following my desire had provided me with the experience I needed to succeed in my next venture. Who knew?

I'm not touting the cliché that everything happens for a reason. Rather, I'm saying that your desires have an important purpose. If I hadn't taken action to put together and promote a band, I wouldn't have been ready to succeed with my first book. Honoring my desires—even though I didn't achieve what I'd initially hoped for—was the key.

Because of experiences like this, I think of moving toward the things I yearn for—even superficial things—as marching orders. They help me know what to do next, and how to spend my energy and time. It's not so hard because it's what I want to do anyway.

Ironically, the important thing is *not* so much whether or not I fulfill a desire, but acknowledging that I have it.

To get there, I have to take the indispensable first step: figure out what I want.

FIGURE OUT WHAT YOU WANT

THIS STEP MAY SOUND OBVIOUS, but acknowledging your desires is not as easy as it sounds. For one thing, desires can be scary, especially if they seem impossible. Just acknowledging your desires requires some courage. Also, as my story about being a singer illustrates, desires change, so it's important to take inventory frequently to monitor what you want now. I have a running list that I add to every few days, and my desires are almost never the same from week to week.

This step is paramount; if you don't know what your desires are, you can't possibly acknowledge that you have them. Then you've separated yourself from even the possibility of having the very things that would bring you the most enjoyment. I love keeping a wish list because seeing my desires in black and white makes them more real than if they just floated around in my head.

Naturally, just knowing what you want won't make those things suddenly appear, but it's a powerful step in that direction.

Chapter 12

SAY WHAT YOU WANT

Listening to your desires will help you articulate them, which is an important step in realizing them. The more you express your desires out loud, the more likely you are to achieve your dreams.

A good receiver recognizes that the people around her want to make her happy and, therefore, want to help her fulfill her desires, so she expresses them freely as a way of allowing others to support her.

You don't have to be certain about every whim before you say it out loud to people who love you, but find someone very safe for your most sacred desires. Sometimes just saying something out loud makes you realize it isn't what you want. After all, it's a woman's prerogative to change her mind.

Ask for what you want and be prepared to get it.

—MAYA ANGELOU

INVITE SUPPORT BY SPEAKING YOUR DESIRES

J UDY KNEW THAT HER DESIRE to buy a house was an authentic one, but after months of looking at houses and trying to come up with a plan to buy, she was ready to give up. "I've racked my brain," she said, "and I can't figure out a way that we can afford to buy a house. I just don't see how it's going to happen."

I reminded Judy that she hadn't racked anyone else's brain yet. I encouraged her to talk about her desire everywhere she went in case a friend or family member could help. So Judy expressed her desire—and her challenges—to her neighbors, her mom, her uncle, her mother-in-law, and her friends. One of her neighbors recommended a terrific Realtor named Haley, who referred Judy to a loan broker named Frank, who came up with a program that required only a small down payment. Judy's mom agreed to loan Judy and her husband part of the down payment, and her husband's boss was willing to advance him his salary to make up the difference. Next, Haley took Judy and her husband house shopping, and they found a wonderful house that they qualified for. They made an offer the same day, it was accepted, and they were in escrow for the one thing she wanted most but was sure she couldn't have—a four-bedroom house in a great neighborhood.

Those same neighbors, family members, and friends who supported Judy through the process were thrilled to celebrate with her when she moved into the house of her dreams. All of this happened because Judy was willing to say what she wanted even though she didn't think she could get it. When she owned those desires, she took the critical first step in attaining what she wanted. Without that, Judy and her family would still be renters because those close to her would not have known how to help.

Just because you express your desire to friends and family members does not mean you have an expectation that those around you will meet your desires—but they might. Let's say you wish you had a bigger home. If you say so out loud, your friends know to keep their ears to the ground so they can tell you when they hear about a roomier place coming available, or about a great Realtor, or about a contractor who builds additions. If you don't express that desire out loud, you'll cheat yourself from receiving from people who just want to help.

You may worry that people will think you're ungrateful if you're always talking about what you want, but remember that desire and gratitude are *not* opposites. You can be very grateful for what you have and still want more as long as you don't confuse desire with entitlement. If you're feeling self-conscious about this, you can always express your gratitude along with your desire, as in, "I'm so grateful to be living in Manhattan. Now I just want to find an apartment that's a little bigger."

Oprah Winfrey did a show about granting wishes, which beautifully illustrated the point of saying your wild, outrageous desires. Oprah's producers approached some women and asked them what they wanted, and several said, "to meet Oprah." Others said, "a new home" or "to have my student loans paid off." Oprah gave each of the women her wish, and when the ones who had wished to meet Oprah found out what she had done for the women who had bigger desires, they were disappointed. "We didn't know we could wish for something like that," they said. But Oprah encouraged them to use this experience as a lesson in dreaming bigger.

See how important it is to know what you want, independent of what anyone else thinks is possible?

I know it seems more practical not to waste time saying you want things that you can't have, but if you don't even admit that you want them, you'll certainly never get them. Therefore, even if you're terrified that you're desires will make you seem foolish when you can't get them, find the courage to honor them anyway.

> *Perhaps it would be a good idea, fantastic as it sounds, to muffle every telephone, stop every motor, and halt all activity for an hour some day, to give people a chance to ponder for a few minutes on what it is all about, why they are living and what they really want.*
>
> —James Truslow Adams

Be Straight and You Won't Manipulate

"Don't tell anybody what you wished for or it won't come true," someone probably whispered to you when you were a child. But whoever started that familiar myth had it backward. Saying what you wish out loud is not only more fun than keeping it a secret, it makes your wish *more likely* to come true. That's because once other people know your wish, they just might be able to help you make it happen. Adding the weight of your words also makes a desire more real than it was before you breathed it into existence; it shows that you value your desires, which gives them more importance than the things you don't say out loud.

As a child you might have heard lots of messages about how you should *not* express your desires. Maybe you were told to stop being so self-centered, to think of people who had less, or to be polite and not ask for things. At the grocery store recently, I heard a dad tell his kids that if they asked him for one more thing, he was going to put them in time-out. That would go a long way toward making me think twice before vocalizing what I wanted.

Perhaps the most important reason to say your desire out loud is to articulate it to yourself. Expressing your desires clearly is a lot better than keeping them under your breath and manipulating to get them, which is what happens when you subvert your desires. For instance, saying, "I wish I had a whole room for doing crafts" is a pure expression of desire. Saying, "Why don't you clean the junk out of that room since you're not using it for anything important," is an unpleasant criticism and a manipulation designed to achieve the same end: an extra room for you to use. The pure expression will be more effective every time, but it requires that you own your desires. Once you've expressed them, you won't even be tempted to say something negative or critical because you won't need to. You've already been direct, which is the most effective way to communicate.

Unless you know what you want, you can't ask for it.

—EMMA ALBANI

SAYING WHAT YOU WANT MAKES YOU MORE BEAUTIFUL

SOME WOMEN WORRY that announcing their desires will make them seem arrogant or self-centered, but just the opposite is true. Knowing what you want and saying it is a sign of confidence.

It actually makes you more attractive.

One woman hadn't even made the first payment on her student loans from nursing school before she realized that she really wanted to be a hairdresser and began going to beauty school instead. Today, she's a successful hair stylist whose vivacity and passion for her work make her one of the most beautiful women I know. The spark that makes her so appealing would be lacking if she were trudging through life in the wrong profession.

Think how appealing it is to be around someone who definitely knows she wants to go dance the tango, start a million-dollar business, or learn to carve ice sculptures. Now compare that to someone who says, "I'll go along with whatever you want to do" or "I don't care what we do." Such a woman is negating her own desires, which is not attractive. She lacks joie de vivre because she's apathetic.

Granted, you may not want to tango, start a company, or make ice sculptures, but even so, being with someone who is decisive is appealing. When she expresses her desires, it gives you the freedom to express yours. You can say, "I had something else in mind," or you can find a way to do both. Then you're not left guessing what the other person really wanted to do or if she is having a good time.

Certainty and decisiveness are attractive qualities.

Just don't give up trying to do what you really want to do. Where there is love and inspiration, I don't think you can go wrong.

—ELLA FITZGERALD

SECRET DESIRES CAN DRIVE YOUR LOVED ONES CRAZY

I F YOU THINK what you want will make someone else feel bad, you may be tempted to keep it secret. But the danger of *not* expressing those desires cleanly is great because the people who would most like to see you happy get confused.

That's exactly how Janet and Nick felt when Nick's mother, Lily, came to visit them in their new home. Lily announced that if it was too much trouble for her to stay in their home, she would just go to a hotel. Janet didn't think it was too much trouble to have Lily, and she even offered to let Lily have the bed while she and Nick slept on the couch. But Lily protested, "Oh no, I don't want to inconvenience anybody."

Janet felt rejected. She was frustrated trying to persuade Lily that her comfort was a gift that was pleasurable to bestow. If Lily had just said, "As much as I like seeing you, I want to stay in a hotel so I have my own space. I'll stay nearby so that we don't miss out on any time together," Janet wouldn't have felt hurt, or as if her hospitality was being dismissed.

In the end, Janet and Nick spent time and energy accommodating someone who didn't want to be accommodated in the first place. How frustrating and unsatisfying for everyone involved.

I claim the right to contradict myself. I don't want to deprive myself of the right to talk nonsense, and I ask humbly to be allowed to be wrong sometimes.

—Federico Fellini

Your Desires Are Not Set in Concrete

Jo Anne told a group of friends that she wanted to get her master's degree. As soon as she said it, she realized the idea of going back to school sounded dreary to her. She didn't want to appear wishy-washy, so she stuck to her original statement even when her best friend said, "How will that help you with your dream of becoming a painter?"

Another friend e-mailed Jo Anne about a great part-time graduate program on the Internet. The next time the group was together, Jo Anne's friends asked her if she had investigated the course, but she hadn't. Several months went by, and Jo Anne still hadn't lifted one finger toward getting that degree because it wasn't what she wanted.

Finally, Jo Anne admitted to her friends that her parents wanted her to get more education, but that she didn't want to.

Of course her friends didn't think any less of Jo Anne for exploring an idea out loud. In fact, saying it out loud helped her get clear on her deeper desire to be a painter. As soon as she admitted that was what she wanted, she was able to receive something much more valuable from her friends: help and support achieving her true desire.

Along those lines, there's nothing wrong with expressing a desire that's only a passing whim. For instance, Scott introduced me to a friend of his, who told me she was interested in writing a book. Later, Scott told me he was embarrassed that his friend had said she wanted to be a writer when she'd never written anything in her life. Hearing this information didn't make me take her any less seriously, though, because I know that desires change and even sprout unexpectedly. I thought she was courageous to say what she wanted, and I secretly hoped that she would succeed. If she had come back and asked me for more advice about writing, I would have felt honored, and she would have received the help of a bestselling author.

That's how compelling it is when someone knows what she wants.

SAY WHAT YOU WANT TO SOMEONE SAFE

--------⟨∿⟩--------

NATURALLY, YOU DON'T WANT to tell your sacred desires to just anybody. Some people might criticize you for wanting too much; others might squelch your aspirations by suggesting that you can't have what you want. The more dear the desire is to you, the more scary it will feel to say it out loud. Therefore, find someone whom you trust who will honor your desires just as you do.

Even when you have a supportive audience, it takes some courage to tell someone else what you want. If you've been taught to be modest, for instance, you might feel awkward admitting that you want to be a millionaire or a fashion model. If your desire is adventurous, like becoming a movie star or climbing Mount Everest, the desire itself might be intimidating.

Eva had just such a desire: She wanted to run a marathon. She hesitated to mention it to just anyone because although it had long been her dream, it seemed impossible. Finally, she courageously told the people in her inner circle what she hoped to do, knowing that they would take her seriously and hold her accountable.

Now she could no longer hide from her goal. Once she told her friends she was training to run 26.2 miles, she couldn't just quit when she got bored or wanted to give up. She had to push herself—or else publicly acknowledge defeat and embarrassment. By telling her friends and family that she was training, Eva was not only honoring her desire, she was owning it and setting herself up to receive their support.

It was scary—and exhilarating—but it was worth it when she crossed the finish line with her small fan club cheering her on the sidelines.

Chapter 13

✧

ADMIT THAT YOU GOOFED AND APOLOGIZE FOR YOUR PART

A gracious woman acknowledges her errors.

Admitting a mistake requires courage and humility. Being defensive about it isolates you and prevents you from receiving forgiveness because defensiveness and forgiveness cannot coexist. So be proactive about acknowledging your errors, even if you feel that there is more to lose than to gain in the short term; in the long term you will receive more forgiveness, acceptance, and grace.

Start by apologizing the next time you are in the wrong—when you've done something to someone else that would have upset you. That can be anything from interrupting someone to forgetting a birthday to initiating a breakup.

When you deliver an apology, take 100 percent accountability by leaving out the words "but" and "if." Saying, "I'm sorry I hurt your feelings," is being accountable. Saying, "I'm sorry if I hurt your feelings," is not.

When something goes wrong, I'm the first to admit it—and the last one to know.

—PAUL SIMON

GOOD RECEIVERS ARE ACCOUNTABLE

I USED TO THINK that if I admitted my mistakes, people would see me as someone who was always making mistakes and committing offenses, but just the opposite is true. In admitting my errors, I earn trust because others see that I'm accountable.

I remember learning this when I first started leading workshops. One of the women in my group, Shawna, told me in private that she was going to have a hard time at the next meeting and would probably cry all the way through the session. I assured her that it was okay to cry at the workshop and that I admired her honesty and courage.

Another woman in the group, Madeline, had a similar concern. I told her, "Don't worry—Shawna said she'll probably be a fountain at the next meeting, so you won't be the only one." Then I went on to tell her that Shawna and her husband hadn't been sexually active for years.

I was trying to make Madeline feel comfortable, but in the process I revealed very personal details about Shawna that I should have kept confidential. Madeline ran into Shawna during the week and brought up the very topic Shawna had thought was only for my ears. Naturally, Shawna was mortified that Madeline knew intimate details of her life.

And she was furious at me for my carelessness, for betraying her confidence.

When I next spoke to Shawna, she confronted me about the incident. I was filled with an awful sinking feeling as I realized what I had done. I wanted to hide. I wanted to go home and forget about the workshop for that night. Of course, there was no escape.

"I'm sorry, Shawna," I said. "I never should have shared personal details about your life with Madeline. I don't normally do that, and I wish I hadn't done it this time. I'll be careful not to do that again." I didn't try to justify my actions by explaining that I was just trying to make Madeline comfortable. That would have been defensive.

Shawna brightened up considerably. She thanked me for taking her concerns seriously. I was certain she would never trust me after that, but to my surprise, she was soon telling me about how she had discovered that the lack of physical intimacy in her marriage was rooted in her own reluctance. She even revealed that she had been a promiscuous teenager while we discussed what might be at the root of the problem.

I was never careless with her trust again.

How did Shawna know she could trust me to keep her secrets in safe hands after such a terrible lapse in judgment?

I was accountable and contrite, and that forced me to stare my shortcomings in the face—in front of Shawna. It was painful and humbling. But it convinced Shawna that I took her feelings seriously, and that made her feel safe enough to take me into her confidence again.

Life is like playing a violin solo in public and learning the instrument as one goes on.

—SAMUEL BUTLER

ADMITTING YOU WERE WRONG IS NOT AS BAD AS YOU THINK

WHEN YOU'RE WILLING to admit you made a mistake, you also put yourself in the position of receiving forgiveness, grace, and compassion.

A few years ago I was in a fender bender at the mall. I had passed a great parking spot and decided to back up—quickly—to get it. That's when I hit the Hilton shuttle bus.

It wasn't a serious accident, but when an insurance adjuster called later to try to discern what happened, I felt there would be trouble if I admitted I was at fault. I didn't know what kind of trouble exactly, but in my mind it was going to be big. So at the conclusion of the interview when he asked me whose fault the accident was, I paused for a very long time. I thought my choices were either to lie to try to protect myself, or to say I had been at fault and enjoy the freedom of not having to defend myself—but risk the consequences.

"Are you still there?" the insurance inspector asked. "It's okay to say you don't know who was at fault," he offered. So that's what I did, and I immediately felt guilty for lying. I felt as if I had deceived a person whose voice and face I knew well—not an anonymous insurance rep in a faraway state.

I felt uncomfortable about my misdeed for days. Knowing that I could have avoided the miserable feeling that was haunting me added insult to my own injury. I had cheated myself out of the relief that would have come if I had just told the guy that I zigged when I should have zagged.

I wasn't fooling anyone anyway—I got a letter a few weeks later saying they found me at fault, which I was. There—I said it. Phew! What a relief.

If I had admitted culpability, I could have saved myself a lot of fretting. I could also have said I was sorry for the mistake and asked for forgiveness from the shuttle driver and the insurance adjuster. I could have received their compassion and understanding—which the man on the phone was offering—and their validation that accidents happen. Instead, I tried to defend myself when I was in the wrong, and that only made me feel guilty and undeserving of forgiveness.

As it turned out, I didn't even have to pay higher insurance premiums or a deductible, so the consequences of being at fault were absolutely nothing. I had wasted my energy agonizing about how to avoid responsibility to protect myself from an imaginary punishment. That's so typical—so often the consequences of admitting we are wrong are far less than we imagine.

YOUR CRITICS WILL BE SPEECHLESS

Accountability *allows you to receive forgiveness.* Once you've taken responsibility for your actions, there's nothing left for someone else to prove, argue against, or criticize. It's done. No one else can point the finger at you, and so you save yourself from being the target of someone else's ire.

If you try to deny your mistakes, you can't receive anything because you're in a defensive posture—you're standing there with your fists up and clenched. You're not likely to be offered a present then, are you? You couldn't accept anything without letting your guard down anyway. If you have your armor on, you're not going to elicit hugs. Even if you get a hug, you'd barely feel it through all that metal. So you're certainly not going to feel compassion or support from those around you when you're defensive.

Whenever anyone at Naomi's critique group brought up even the smallest suggestion for how she could improve her work, she argued the point and defended her choices forcefully. The other members of the group quickly realized that their feedback was inciting only defensiveness instead of graciousness, and they did what anyone would do in response to feeling unappreciated: they stopped trying to help at all. Naomi seemed incapable of admitting that she'd ever been less than perfect. Her lack of accountability made it impossible for her to receive anything from the group—and made her unpopular to boot.

Had Naomi been receptive to hearing the feedback and either accepting or rejecting it on her own, quietly, she would not only have gotten valuable direction, she would have demonstrated a willingness to receive, which would have encouraged others to devote even more of their energy to her growth and success. She also would have been more likable, and would have felt the support that the others in the group were capable of giving her.

There's Nothing Left to Fight About

M_Y DAD HAD A much better response when he sped past a highway patrol car. Before the officer could even signal my dad to pull over, he pulled *himself* over to the side of the highway. When the officer approached the car, he asked my dad why he had pulled over.

"If I were you and someone went speeding by me, I would pull him over, so I thought I'd save you the trouble," my dad told him.

"You were going too fast," the officer chided him.

"You're right—I was, and I shouldn't have been," my dad agreed.

The officer accepted this confession and let my dad off with a warning instead of a citation. After all, my dad had already acknowledged his mistake and expressed remorse, so there was nothing left to fight about. He even got to feel good about keeping his integrity. His accountability made it easy for the cop to forgive him. My dad was happy to receive that forgiveness rather than the fine he might have incurred. If he had waited to be pulled over and hoped the officer hadn't noticed his speeding, he would almost certainly have been fined.

Instead, my dad put himself squarely in a position to receive.

Defensiveness can be downright infuriating to others. The more someone tries to cover up or justify his wrongdoings, the more determined everyone around him is to prove him wrong. When you insist on defending a mistake, it drives a wedge in your friendship. The issue that you're disagreeing about starts to take on a life of its own. Now the original misdeed is overshadowed by your lack of accountability—which chips away at the trust and integrity of a relationship.

All you have to do to put things right again is say, "Mea culpa."

True confession consists of telling our deed in such a way that our soul is changed in the telling of it.

—MAUDE PETRE

No Ifs or Buts About It

WHEN YOU'RE ACCOUNTABLE, you purposely take full responsibility for the consequences of your actions. You do that by saying, "I'm sorry I hurt your feelings" or "I'm sorry that I left the milk on the counter all night," and nothing more. Adding something is usually about wanting to resolve the conflict without having to be truly accountable.

If you offer an apology by saying, "I'm sorry I left the milk out on the counter, but you've done that before, too," you have just lobbed a bomb along with your so-called apology. Launching a counterattack will only make the other person feel defensive or angry all over again. Keep your eye on the ball and apologize for your part only.

You might be tempted to explain the situation by saying, "I'm sorry I hurt your feelings, but I thought you were being greedy to insist that we have all the holiday get-togethers at your house." But guess what? If you do that, you aren't helping to resolve the conflict at all. In the first half of the sentence you've feigned an apology, but in the second half of the sentence you've reinjured the person to whom you were ostensibly making amends. You weren't really making an apology at all but were using the "I'm sorry" the way a boxer feigns fatigue in a boxing match—so he can get a good punch in.

Making matters worse, you are implicitly denying the other person her feelings.

Another variation on this theme is to pretend that you are being accountable by saying, "I'm sorry *if* I hurt your feelings." Since the other person has already said that she's hurt or upset, there's no "if" about it—you said something hurtful. Adding the word "if" is actually a further insult because, in addition to *not* taking responsibility for your words, you imply that what you said shouldn't have hurt her and that she's oversensitive.

Now that you're aware of these pitfalls, you'll want to avoid adding an explanation or any qualifiers to your apologies. To be truly accountable, which will give you a resulting peace and intimacy—there's only one thing to do: swallow the bitter pill of admitting you goofed.

For best results, leave out any ifs, ands, or buts.

Truth, like surgery, may hurt, but it cures.

HAN SUYIN

ADMITTING YOU'RE WRONG IS ATTRACTIVE

A WOMAN WHO LIVED in a small village was famous for making beautiful pottery and rugs. When someone asked her to reveal the secret of how she made such beautiful wares, she told them, "I always make a mistake in the design or the pattern—on purpose—to acknowledge that only God is perfect." Instead of detracting from her work, the imperfections increased the appeal and beauty of her hand-crafted items.

The same is true for your mistakes. When you acknowledge them, they make you more appealing and beautiful. That's partly because your foibles make you human, which means the rest of us can identify and connect with you. It's also partly because it takes confidence to admit you're wrong, and confidence is always attractive.

Ironically, you feel the least confident when you've just made a mistake. But the more you are accountable by owning your mistakes, the more self-assured you seem and therefore become. That self-assurance springs from knowing you're valuable and lovable even though you've made a mistake.

The truth is, everyone has done awful things. Part of what made Princess Diana so popular the world over was her willingness to admit her bad deeds, which showed that despite being a princess, she was vulnerable like the rest of us. She did good things too—like charitable work—but she admitted to having an eating disorder and to being involved in an extramarital affair. She was a stark contrast to Queen Elizabeth, who worked hard to keep up an impeccable image but lost favor with the people when she failed to say anything about Diana's tragic death. England longed for Elizabeth to lead the country by acknowledging the tremendous loss and her own sorrow, but she resisted showing any vulnerability. The more people clamored for her to make a statement, the more tight-lipped—and unpopular—Elizabeth became.

Maybe she just had a hard time admitting she was wrong.

Princess Diana was a great woman. Queen Elizabeth is a great woman. Both lives clearly demonstrate that the woman who made the rugs and pottery is right: Only God is perfect. For the rest of us, there are apologies.

It is so much easier to tell intimate things in the dark.

—William McFee

Get Forgiveness from Yourself

I find myself most attracted to people who have done awful things and lived to tell about them, and most bored by (or frustrated with) people who admit nothing. That's only because I've done awful things myself. Shall I tell you about the time I bounced twelve checks in one month? Or would you rather hear about the time I berated a hapless salesclerk?

Naturally, I'm tempted to keep all of this a secret because I don't want anyone to judge me for my misdeeds. But I don't want to be alone with my secrets either; they only fester into self-judgment and shame. For one thing, I feel terrible when I've done something to hurt someone else, and those feelings of guilt only grow deeper when I keep them hidden in a dark corner of my mind. My self-judgment kicks into overdrive and tries to convince me that I am the only person in the history of the universe who has ever bounced checks.

When I admit to someone else that I've done something I'm not proud of, I find out that I'm not so unusual, that other people have committed similar sins. When my sins are no longer secrets, I can feel good about myself again because I'm just like everybody else—I make mistakes that I have to make amends for. Hearing about other people's shortcomings reminds me that we're all mere mortals and helps me release any judgment I have about myself. Apologizing gives me both the opportunity to free myself from shame and the appearance of being more confident and therefore more attractive.

Would you rather hear about someone's most embarrassing moment, or how virtuous she is? The times she was busted in school, or the times she made the honor roll? The time he was fired or his consistently perfect performance reviews? I'm more interested in hearing about other people's blunders—not because I take satisfaction from their misery but because I identify with their mistakes. Their honesty and vulnerability make them approachable, interesting, and safe to talk to. Such people are not defensive—they're authentic. They've learned to laugh at their mistakes, which is attractive. So not only does owning your mistakes and apologizing make you feel better on the inside, it also makes you look better on the outside.

Apologies Are Free, So Spread Them Around

You may have been taught—as many women are—not to apologize.

The thinking goes like this: In the past women subverted their own needs, desires, and opinions so instinctively that if they needed something as basic as a bathroom break, wanted something inconvenient, or had a differing opinion, they would begin their sentence with an apology. As a result, many people say that women should never apologize because it represses their feelings and makes their desires seem unimportant.

However, another way to look at apologies is that they are a powerful way of showing respect and of expressing a spirit of cooperation.

Let's say you called a friend a big flake because she canceled at the last minute when the two of you had plans to go to a concert. Now the air between you is thick with tension, and you're thinking that she should apologize, since she *did* stand you up and she *is* a flake. You might think that apologizing for your part—insulting her—would make you weak and would make it seem okay that she didn't keep her commitment. But apologizing doesn't make you weak. *Not* apologizing would be dismissive of your friend; although it's understandable that you would be hurt and angry, your response to her was also hurtful. When you apologize for your part, you're not saying the other person doesn't have culpability—just that you want to clean up your side of the street. It's a way of saying that the relationship with your friend is more important to you than this latest incident.

You build intimacy and a culture of mutual respect when you apologize. It makes you polite—not pathetic. None of us is perfect all the time, but when you apologize after a mistake, you reopen the door to intimacy.

IT TAKES TWO TO TANGO

My friend Carla has a policy of making apologies when she wants an apology. This is not a manipulation, as in, "If I apologize then they'll apologize too, and I'll get what I want." Rather, she reviews the situation for ways that she has contributed to a conflict because she knows that conflicts are hardly ever one-sided.

So, when Carla finds herself wanting an apology, she knows she has to ask herself, "What did I do that I owe an apology for?" Once she figures it out and makes her amends, she very often gets an apology in return. By looking for her part in the situation, she puts herself squarely in the position to receive amends.

When you feel wronged, the temptation is to look at what someone else did to you. Instead, consider how you may have offended her. Of course, you can't make anyone apologize, but you can clear the way for reconciliation by taking responsibility for your part.

I read about a high school music teacher who reached the same conclusion. He was upset with his students because they had come late or not at all to a special concert that he had arranged for them to hear. He was indignant. His first instinct was to lecture them and complain, but he knew they wouldn't listen if he did. Next he tried to convince himself that it was their loss. That approach denied his own emotional investment in his students. What he had really wanted was for the kids to see what he considered a great performance. Finally, he asked himself what his part in the conflict was, and although it was difficult to face, he realized he did have a small part in it.

Instead of berating his students, he said, "I am sorry that I failed you regarding this concert. I meant to tell you how excited I was, what a great opportunity it would be, and how much I thought you would enjoy the performance, but I must not have done that very well, and now most of you have missed the performance. I am sorry about that. Next time, I'll do better."

The students were moved by his confession—and vulnerability—and began apologizing to him for not attending the concert. Instead of feeling hurt and angry about his students' poor attitude, the teacher discovered that the kids held him in high enough regard to say they were sorry for *their* part. Harmony and camaraderie were restored to his classroom.

By making his apology to the class, he put himself squarely in a position to receive those apologies from his students.

Some people might see his actions as a manipulation or an attempt to make the students feel guilty, but he didn't tell them they were bad or should be ashamed. He wasn't seeking anything from the kids. He didn't make himself a victim by taking responsibility for his small part—quite the opposite. He was simply accountable for the only thing you can be accountable for—his own actions and attitude. No more, no less.

You may be nervous—just as I was—to talk about your mistakes and apologize when you think you have been wronged, but if what you want is to be more confident, have better intimacy, and attract more gifts, I can think of nothing more powerful than accountability.

In revealing an error you are also revealing your self-confidence; you are showing that you believe enough in yourself to know that one mistake isn't going to make anyone think less of you—or make you think less of yourself. This projection of self-confidence is one of the best beauty secrets in the world.

Chapter 14

❧

GIVE UP GUILT

Guilt is an indulgence. You can't be gracious or receptive when you're splashing around in a puddle of guilt because receptivity requires self-love and guilt fills you with the opposite—self-reproach. Therefore, to increase your capacity to receive, make a decision to stop reacting out of guilt.

Instead of apologizing for a single transgression over and over, let one sincere apology be enough.

Accept forgiveness the first time it's offered by dropping the topic.

If forgiveness is not offered, forgive yourself by letting go of the NET (needless emotional turmoil) of saying to yourself, "If only I didn't . . ." or "I'm so awful for . . ." Replace this conversation in your head with sentences like, "From now on . . ." or "In the future . . ."

If you feel guilty when you receive a gift, remind yourself that you deserve beautiful things and that to reject them is to deny the giver the pleasure of giving to you.

Guilt binds us to the darkest parts of ourselves. It's a connection to our weakness, our shame, and our unforgiveness. The smallest part of ourselves feeds on it. Inaction nourishes it. When we feel guilty, we stay small-minded, our lower thoughts are in control.

—ELISABETH KÜBLER-ROSS

"GUILT IS THE GIFT THAT KEEPS ON GIVING"

THAT'S WHAT ERMA BOMBECK SAID, and I know just what she means.

Psychiatrist Karl Menninger tells the story of a man who conducted an experiment from a street corner in Chicago. The man waited for a while, then raised his arm to point at someone randomly passing by and said, "Guilty!" He waited a while longer and did it again. Menninger reported that the experiment was eerie because once accused, people would stare at the man, then look away and rush off. One man turned to someone else and said, "How did he know?"

Many people have feelings of guilt perpetually bubbling right under the surface. That's because everyone has done something wrong, and all of us carry around with us judgments about ourselves. But that doesn't mean you have to feel guilty all the time.

In some ways, guilt seems involuntary. It wells up and hijacks your thoughts. It inspires free-floating messages like

"You're such a bad mother" or "You're a slob." These get replayed in your head until you internalize the message and come to see yourself as inadequate. Or it's the result of something specific you've done that you regret, as in, "I shouldn't have yelled at my best friend" or "I should have gone to the gym last night instead of watching TV."

But guilt isn't a feeling at all—it's a thought that's full of judgment: *You are bad.* When that judgment is allowed to fester the result is guilt—a debilitating, paralyzing condemnation of self.

Since we can control our thoughts, we are in control of our own guilt and how much we indulge in it. Guilt, therefore, is a choice, and when we say we're feeling guilty, what we really mean is that we've decided to wallow in a mistake. We're replaying that mistake repeatedly in our minds, wasting our energy on something that's over, but still holding on to the negativity.

If the root of the guilt is our own self-criticism, then we're going to get out a microscope and hyper-focus on what we perceive as our shortcomings with the goal of making ourselves feel bad.

I've done this myself. Once, during a close volleyball game, I was out of position and let the ball hit the ground, giving the other team a point. I was *very* upset with myself. Instead of focusing on receiving the next serve, I was still thinking about the play that I had just missed and how I had let my team down. I was full of judgment for myself and obsessively replayed the whole scenario in my mind repeatedly. What was I doing out of position? I wondered to myself guiltily. I know better than that. That was terrible. As you can imagine, when the next serve arrived, I was so distracted and discombobulated from wallowing in guilt about my previous mistake that I bungled the pass. Telling myself how awful I had been had only hurt my team and me further.

That's why guilt is an indulgence that you can't afford. Instead of thinking about how you can improve or how you can avoid doing the same thing in the future, guilt keeps you stuck in the mud. When you choose guilt, you make yourself a victim—a wretch who did something wrong and can't hold her head up because of it. Instead of doing something constructive, you become passive.

The key to switching from guilt to receiving forgiveness after you've done something regrettable is simply to say "I'm sorry"—then let it go.

My mother could make anybody feel guilty—she used to get letters of apology from people she didn't even know.

—JOAN RIVERS

YOU'RE THE DEEJAY OF YOUR OWN HEAD

FORTUNATELY, GUILT ISN'T INVOLUNTARY.

You're the deejay of your head: you decide which recordings to play in there. So stop spinning records that make you feel bad. You might hear the beginnings of some songs of torment popping up in the rotation from time to time, but the key is not to press the "play" button—or, at the very least, don't hit "repeat."

For instance, let's say you suddenly realize you've missed your sister's birthday and you start to give yourself a guilt trip about it. Since wallowing in guilt isn't going to help you or your sister, you could just decide to stop playing that tape altogether and focus on something that would help the person you've wronged.

So the guilt trip might sound like this:

"Oh no! I missed my sister's birthday. I should have gotten her something—or at least called. I am such a jerk—what is wrong with me? Now it's too late, and I just look like a complete flake. I am a flake. I blew it!" (Repeat ad nauseam.)

Cutting your guilt trip short might sound like this:

"Oh no! I missed my sister's birthday! I should have gotten her something—or at least called. I wish I hadn't forgotten. It's too late to celebrate on the actual day, but I can get her a card now and send it. I'll tell her I'm sorry for missing her day. These things happen. I hope she understands."

After having the first conversation with yourself, you wouldn't be very open to receiving her forgiveness. How could you be? No one could get a word in. But if you've had the second conversation with yourself, you would probably be open to receiving sympathy or reassurance.

One good way to tell if you're wallowing in guilt is to ask yourself if you're thinking about something you have the power to change. If not, then it's time to put on a new record.

If you're thinking about something that you can change, then change it—or accept it as it is. Make peace with yourself somehow or you'll miss out on receiving the gifts, help, and compliments you could have had.

IF ONE APOLOGY IS GOOD,
MORE IS BETTER, RIGHT?

I THOUGHT SO.

You should have heard me trying to apologize to a friend when I nearly burned down her bathroom. I had left my skirt on the counter too close to a candle after I changed into a swimsuit; while we sat in her backyard spa, the skirt caught on fire and set off the smoke alarm. Naturally, I felt very guilty when the flames damaged my friend's new wallpaper and set off the smoke alarm, so I offered to pay for the damage. I said I was sorry again and again. I thought that would alleviate the pain of my guilt, but it didn't. It certainly didn't lessen my friend's annoyance at putting her bathroom back together.

Even if my friend had said, "Laura, I know you didn't mean to burn my bathroom wall, and I forgive you," I probably wouldn't have been able to take that in and let the incident go. I was too busy punishing myself. On some level I believed that by continuing to suffer I was compensating for my crime.

I'm not the only one with the crazy misconception that guilt serves some important purpose.

Lisa was a student in my marriage workshop. We were talking about how to give up trying to control your husband—what he wears, what he eats, when he takes out the trash, etc. The more we talked, the more embarrassed and agitated Lisa became as she started to see that she constantly berated, demeaned, and emasculated her husband without realizing it. "I'm beginning to see just how controlling I've been," she told us, "and I feel awful about it." Lisa told us that there was no end to the nagging, dismissing, and disrespectful things she had said to her husband during their ten years of marriage. She felt tremendous regret and guilt.

Armed with her new perspective, Lisa went home and apologized to her husband for all her years of bad behavior. Her husband, Bruce, appreciated her heartfelt apology and said, "You weren't that bad." But Lisa insisted that she had been horrible and asked her husband to forgive her. Bruce quickly said, "I forgive you," at which point he probably hoped the conversation might end since there was no pleasure for him in seeing his wife uncomfortable with the pain of remorse, nor did he care to rehash the times she had dismissed or demeaned him.

Bruce wanted to be able to forgive his wife and move on—to enjoy her company instead of watching her beat herself. He suggested they work a crossword puzzle together, but Lisa wanted to talk some more about how awful she felt, how much she realized now that she had been wrong, how much she regretted her behavior. Finally Bruce wandered off to watch TV, so Lisa called a girlfriend to tell her how horrible she had been. Later she apologized to Bruce a few more times.

Perhaps Lisa also believed on some level that if she wallowed in regret for how she had treated her husband, she would atone for her terrible behavior. But Lisa's actions spoke louder than her words. Instead of being more considerate of her husband, she dismissed him again when he was trying to give her something precious: forgiveness.

Perhaps she felt no one would believe that she was contrite unless she made a big deal about it. Or maybe feeling guilty was easier for her than having to change her behavior. But her discomfort didn't help anyone. In fact, repeatedly moaning about how awful she'd been was causing everyone else around her—including her husband—to suffer her unpleasant self-flagellation. Lisa's response to guilt was entirely self-centered, which is never appealing. Instead of having his wife's respect and attention, Bruce ended up feeling annoyed because she just wasn't listening to him. Worst of all, Lisa missed a chance to receive her husband's generous forgiveness.

Too bad she didn't just take what was being offered: a complete pardon with no strings attached.

I often see people indulging in the awful, agonizing feeling of guilt, as if it alleviates the pain of the person they offended.

So let's set the record straight: Guilt doesn't do anything beneficial for anyone. Guilt is not what keeps you from doing bad things—your morals do that, or sometimes the threat of being punished. Cringing with guilt doesn't build houses, heal sick people, or keep you warm.

Guilt is a big, fat waste of energy.

In addition to making you feel bad, guilt is also unattractive because it contributes to feelings of unworthiness and insecurity. When you're consumed with guilt, you can't receive anything—especially forgiveness.

That was my experience with that volleyball game when I made two errors in a row during a close match. Instead of shaking it off and going back to enjoying the game, I suddenly felt undeserving of being on the team. I worried that the other players were disappointed with me, when really they probably weren't thinking about me at all. My sudden bout of insecurity had to do with my own judgments, not those of anyone around me. But the lack of confidence showed in my playing, my expression, and my posture. Nobody wants to be around someone so full of self-doubt that she needs reassurance to stop feeling anxious. It certainly isn't attractive.

A lot of guilt comes from the feeling that we have more influence than we really do.

—DAN GOTTLIEB

YOUR WORDS COUNT THE FIRST TIME

REGARDLESS OF THE SEVERITY of the crime, if you're offered forgiveness, a good receiver accepts. To do any less is to indulge your guilt—the voices that say you are bad—instead of choosing intimacy, confidence, and tenderness from the person who is saying, "You are forgiven."

If you apologize *after* someone has forgiven you, it demonstrates that you either didn't hear them or that you're not receiving the forgiveness. Otherwise, apologizing again would be unnecessary.

If you let guilt prevent you from receiving forgiveness, you never get the closure on the incident and move on.

And consider this: As you continue to ask to be forgiven, you are actually looking to the person you already injured to make you feel better.

That's what happened to Carla when the freelancer she had hired to design an important brochure called to say that he wouldn't be taking on the project that he had committed to after all. Carla was angry and disappointed, knowing that his eleventh-hour change of heart was going to result in her having to work longer and call in more portfolios to find someone in a hurry.

"Listen, I'm really sorry about the inconvenience of this," the designer apologized. "I hope you're not angry."

"Thank you. I accept your apology." Carla sighed.

"I'm really sorry about this," he said again. "I hope it doesn't cause you any difficulty."

"It will cause me difficulty," Carla said straightforwardly, thinking of the pressure of her looming deadline.

The man apologized several more times before Carla finally said, "I have nothing more to say to you," and ended the call.

"I had the distinct feeling that he wanted me to assuage his guilt by telling him it was okay, but it wasn't okay with me," Carla told me. "I accepted his apology immediately, so repeating the apology made me feel badgered into taking care of his emotional needs, which I had no interest in doing."

In other words, he wanted the very person whom he had injured and who was going to suffer the most as a result of his not keeping his commitment to make him feel better. That's what it feels like to the other person when you apologize more than once.

Although you may be tempted at times to apologize for something repeatedly, once really is enough. A confident woman knows that her words count the first time, but even if you don't always feel that way, you can act as if you do. The fake-it-till-you-make-it approach is to refrain from overapologizing as a discipline, even when guilt is screaming at you to say you're sorry one more time. This can be especially painful if someone you've apologized to is still mad at you or hasn't offered forgiveness. I have a terrible time sitting still when that happens because I urgently want to restore the peace to alleviate—you guessed it—my guilt. I think that getting the other person's forgiveness—which I have no control over—will make me feel better.

But I'm the only person who can alleviate my guilt. Sure, it would be a relief to have forgiveness, but you can't force that. You can ask, "Will you forgive me? Do you still like me?"

If the answer is no, you can always forgive yourself. At least you know you've done your part.

The rest is beyond your control.

Nina discovered this when she had the misfortune to be driving around the corner just as the neighbor's dog ran in the street. Nina had no time to react, and the dog was killed instantly. The neighbor was understandably upset, and Nina—an avid animal lover—was, too. Nina apologized to her neighbor about the accident, but the neighbor stiffened and walked away. Then it was up to Nina to forgive herself.

She went in the house, made herself a cup of hot cocoa, and had a good cry. She reminded herself that she could not have avoided hitting the dog, and that it was just an accident—tragic, yes—but not unforgivable. She was cordial to the neighbor after that, but never again offered an apology because she knew that one really was enough.

Do not lose courage in considering your own imperfections, but instantly set about remedying them—every day begin the task anew.

—SAINT FRANCIS DE SALES

CONTRITION LEADS TO CHANGE

FEELING GUILTY ISN'T HELPING you atone for anything, but it is helping you avoid the real problem, which is that something needs to change. And that something is probably you.

Guilt doesn't make you change—it makes you annoying.

You're not looking the problem in the face and making a plan for how you can do better next time. You're just moaning and that's it.

Making amends through action always trumps the passivity of guilt and serves to improve the emotional connections with those you've trampled. Instead of making multiple apologies for your misdeeds, make a single apology and spend the rest of your energy on either contrition or acceptance.

Contrition means that you feel genuinely sorry for your mistakes, and it can't help but lead you to making a change for the better. For instance, if you feel terrible for always running late, you would make a conscious effort to be punctual as a way of making amends to those who have waited for you in the past. If you left the kitchen such a mess that your roommate had to clean up, you would vow to do your dishes promptly in the future. If you've hurt a loved one's feelings, you can show contrition by reassuring him of your caring and affection.

Choosing contrition over guilt means you say only "I'm sorry," then make the necessary changes to avoid repeating the incident. If the other person has accepted your apology and you keep going on and on about your guilt, you're not accepting the forgiveness—you're shutting out the gift of being forgiven. That, in the end, will hurt the intimacy with the other person.

Chapter 15

❖

ACCEPT APOLOGIES

When someone apologizes to you, don't interrupt. Allow her to finish articulating her thoughts, then thank her and tell her that you accept the apology—if you do. If you're still angry or feel that there's still unfinished business, thank the person for making amends and calmly and clearly tell her that you're still upset.

Notice how people often dismiss apologies by interrupting the person who is apologizing with a quick, "Don't worry about it," or "That's okay." Notice, too, the sting, however slight, that you feel when your apology is rebuffed before you can even finish offering it.

If you feel that in general people don't apologize to you, take a step back and ask yourself if you are unwittingly rejecting their amends by automatically saying, "Never mind." That's as good as putting a sock in their apology. You've put up your hand to their words and shut yourself down to receiving their kindness.

The first step to receiving apologies is to recognize that you deserve them, and that receiving amends will foster a connection between you and others—from your husband to your coworker to the bus driver. Intimacy grows from apologies because they require you to accept other people's tenderness and to share vulnerability with them.

When you learn to say, "Thank you. Apology accepted," you encourage others to treat you with respect, and to apologize to you knowing that you will accept it—not dismiss it.

> *The society of women is the element of good manners.*
>
> —JOHANN WOLFGANG VON GOETHE

THE HIGH PRICE OF MAKING NICE

WOMEN ARE EXPERTS AT MAKING NICE.

Making nice prevents friction and fighting in families and among friends, and that's comforting. However, sometimes in the rush to be done with the tension from an unpleasant or hurtful interaction, we reject the offer of an apology and, therefore, reject the very person with whom we are trying to reconcile.

Here's what I mean: Let's say you're meeting a friend for lunch, and she's late. You might start to wonder if you have the wrong date, or maybe the wrong spot. You could worry that she's been held up because she was in an accident.

By the time she shows up, you probably feel relieved that you have the right time and place and that she's okay.

But you're also irritated.

Doesn't she respect my time and how busy I am? you might think. Your friend, however, is apologetic about not meeting you on time and she repeatedly says she is sorry. Chances are that you decide to "make nice" by pretending that nothing happened. That's when you tell her, "That's okay," and wave your hand to make the whole problem go away. You might even interrupt her midapology to tell her to forget about it. After all, if you're like many women, your immediate goal is to get past the tension. You want to enjoy your lunch with her, and you don't want to harp on your hurt feelings or her guilt—that's too uncomfortable.

You also want her to like you and to know that you understand about making nice. That's really important to most women, including me.

But when you say, "That's okay" or "Don't worry about it," or "It was nothing," you've actually just rejected your friend's amends and been disrespectful to yourself. Implicit in her apology is the message: "Your time is important, and I regret that I made you wait. Please accept my apology." By rejecting the apology, you're sending a message: "It's okay to keep me waiting." Apologizing a second time might be her way of saying, "No, no—your time is important and I *do* owe you an apology for wasting yours." Continuing to reject those words dismisses her. Not only have you interrupted her and pooh-poohed what she is saying, but you have also dismissed her view of you as someone who deserves consideration and respect.

In waving off her apology, you are rejecting *her*. And you are minimizing yourself. Rejection—no matter how small—never feels good, and poor receiving is never attractive. So instead of smoothing things over, you've just widened the chasm between you and your friend by refusing what she's offering.

REHEARSE YOUR ACCEPTANCE SPEECH

JUST AS WITH DISMISSING COMPLIMENTS, refusing an apology hurts the intimacy in your relationships and reveals a lack of self-worth. It's as if you're saying, "You don't have to apologize to me when you mistreat me because I'm not that important. Even though I've been wronged in some way, I don't want you to feel bad or have to make amends." That's a message of low self-esteem.

Therefore, a self-respecting woman responds to an apology first with a simple "thank you." If she is ready to accept the apology, she'll say that, too. I use these words: "Thank you for that. I accept your apology" or "I appreciate that. Apology accepted." Such a reception demonstrates confidence because it shows that you know you deserve consideration and thoughtfulness. Saying, "That's okay," when someone apologizes to you is the same as saying, "You don't have to worry about wasting my time because my time isn't that important anyway" or "I'm not upset that you forgot my birthday because it's not such a special day." No confident woman would say those things because she is self-assured enough to know that her time is valuable and that her birthday is special.

When I first noticed that I was rejecting apologies, I vowed that I would stop saying, "That's okay," and start thanking people when they said they were sorry. At first, I wasn't very good at it. I'd get an apology, and before I knew it I had said, "No problem." Finally, I remembered to receive apologies, but I found that just saying thanks wasn't enough to resolve the conversation. Resolution came when I actively let the person know that I had not only received the apology but also accepted it.

I discovered this when I was talking to a friend who had taken several days to return a phone call. He apologized profusely, so after I let him finish I said, "Thank you for the apology. I was wondering what happened to you." I was ready to move on, but he apologized again, so I thanked him again, and tried to talk about something else, but I knew that the incident felt unfinished. Later in the conversation, he brought up his lapse yet again by saying, "So you accept my apology?" Once I said, "Yes, I accept your apology," the conversation felt complete for both of us. Just knowing that I heard his apology wasn't enough; my friend wanted to make sure that I was not still upset—that I wouldn't harbor a resentment. Our relationship didn't feel right to him until he heard that I not only received but also *accepted* his apology.

Forgiveness does not change the past, but it does enlarge the future.

—PAUL BOESE

FIRST RECEIVE, THEN ACCEPT OR REJECT AN APOLOGY

I F YOU'RE IN THE HABIT OF DISMISSING APOLOGIES, you may feel awkward when you first practice receiving one. That's because receiving an apology will make you feel vulnerable.

By thanking someone for an apology, you're acknowledging that one was due; you're admitting that you felt hurt or slighted in some way—and to do so is to admit a tenderness.

When I accepted an apology from my friend who didn't return my calls, I was saying, albeit in shorthand, "I felt neglected and hurt when I didn't hear from you for three days. I was afraid that I was unimportant to you." That's a very tender message, but conveying it showed that I was human and had enough courage and strength to reveal a bruise. That's the vulnerability. I could have pretended that I'm not vulnerable by dismissing his apology with the words, "That's all right—forget it." But that wouldn't be as authentic or have been as good for our friendship, since revealing the tenderness is what allows me to connect to others.

The person who's doing the apologizing is also revealing *his* vulnerability. He is saying, "I admit I was wrong" or "I was an inconsiderate jerk." If you match his tenderness, it naturally causes a pleasant connection between you. So now both of you are vulnerable—you for admitting your hurt, him for acknowledging his mistake. When two people are vulnerable together, each knows that the other trusts him. That's an honor that you don't get from just anyone.

You are in the exact position of a thief who's been caught red-handed and isn't sorry he stole but is terribly, terribly sorry he's going to jail.

—RHETT BUTLER TO SCARLET O'HARA IN GONE WITH THE WIND

NOT ALL APOLOGIES ARE ACCEPTABLE

WHEN YOU ACCEPT AN APOLOGY, you are implying that you won't be resentful or let your hurt fester. You're saying that you realize the apologizer is only human, and that the wound wasn't fatal to your relationship. That's very different from saying, "That's okay," which pretends that nothing happened.

A confident woman doesn't dismiss apologies, but she doesn't automatically accept them either. Rather, she honors herself by expressing how she feels at the moment.

When you get an apology for something about which you are still unresolved, you may have a hard time receiving the apology. You may be tempted to punish the person who's wronged you by rejecting her peace offering. While there's no gracious way to reject someone's apology, you can *delay* accepting an apology if you're just not ready.

For example, you might say, "This is pretty upsetting to me, and I appreciate your apologizing, but I'm going to need some time to get over this." You haven't rejected the apology or the intimacy that person is trying to offer, but you have honored your feelings, which is an important part of maintaining self-esteem and being and appearing confident. In this circumstance, you would want to come back to the person later and say, "I wanted to let you know I accept your apology," as a way of restoring the relationship.

Sometimes you have to *reject* an apology to honor yourself. For instance, if your boyfriend apologized for standing you up for the umpteenth time, a self-respecting woman would have to refuse his apology because it lacks credibility. Rejecting his apology would mean rejecting intimacy with that man, which would in turn help clear the space for a man who treats you well.

That's exactly what happened with Kay and Wayne. They had been engaged for years, but Kay could never get Wayne to set a date. Deep down she knew that he was never going to marry her, that he had bought her a ring only to prolong the relationship without making a real commitment. When some of her girlfriends encouraged her to either set a date or give back the ring and break off the relationship, she knew it was time to make a decision. She said to Wayne, "I'm really looking forward to getting married, and I want to set a date so I can start planning. How is May of next year?"

Wayne looked uncomfortable and shifted in his chair as he said, "There's so much going on right now with my job—I just don't think it's a good time."

"We've waited a long time already," Kay said. "I don't want to wait forever."

"I'm sorry, but now just isn't a good time," he told her.

"I'm so disappointed to hear that," she said. "I thought when you proposed and gave me this ring that meant that we would be husband and wife soon. But I see now that wasn't your intent. It's so sad."

"I'm sorry you're disappointed," he responded quickly. "We'll get married someday, just not now. Don't be upset, Kay."

But Kay *was* upset. She knew that this apology wasn't acceptable to her. She took off her ring and returned it to Wayne on the spot, which freed her up to meet Tony six months later. After about a year of dating, she and Tony were married in a park overlooking a canyon.

See how important it is to reject apologies to honor yourself?

IF YOU HAVEN'T BEEN WRONGED, IT'S RIGHT TO REJECT AN APOLOGY

ANOTHER REASON YOU MIGHT REJECT an apology is if you weren't owed one in the first place. Just as you wouldn't issue an apology if you didn't have anything to apologize for, you need not accept an apology from someone who hasn't slighted you in the least.

I recently apologized to a lawyer I had been working with on a business venture that failed. I had persuaded him to become involved, and when the project fizzled and profits were nil, I felt responsible for his having wasted his time. When I said I was sorry that things hadn't worked out, he responded by rejecting my apology. He said, "I don't accept your apology, because that's just how business goes sometimes. Not every venture is successful, and that's not your fault. I got involved because I wanted to get involved, so I reject your apology."

In this case, hearing that he didn't accept my apology felt wonderful because I knew that he felt I hadn't hurt him a bit. Also, he was acknowledging that things hadn't gone the way we had hoped—but that he knew I couldn't control the outcome. He was clear that there was a difference between my hurting him and both of us being disappointed by circumstances, and that clarity was a gift for me.

It wouldn't have been the same if he had said, "No worries," or "Don't even think about it." He didn't *dismiss* my apology—he took it very seriously *and then* refused it. If he had just brushed me off, I would have felt unheard. His response was an acknowledgment of our shared disappointment. I walked away knowing that a valuable colleague still valued me.

That said, I urge you to be very cautious about rejecting apologies. Remember that even if the transgression was minuscule, you are still deserving of an amends, so try to receive it graciously.

RECEIVING APOLOGIES INCREASES YOUR CONFIDENCE

YOU MAY FEEL STRANGE thanking someone for an apology, but what you're really saying is that you're grateful for his or her consideration of your feelings. As with all gratitude, you're encouraging the other person to continue treating you respectfully. Hearing yourself utter the words "Thank you—apology accepted" will serve to remind you that you are worthy of the courtesy of an apology whenever you have been slighted.

When you're honoring your own self-worth, you feel more deserving of good treatment, and that feeling translates into an air of self-assurance that everyone who meets you can see.

That's just one more way that becoming a gracious receiver will improve your confidence.

Chapter 16

❖

NEVER COMPLAIN

When you complain (the opposite of expressing gratitude) you are focusing on what's not going well; that
alone will keep you from receiving. Complaining keeps
you stuck in the situation that has ignited your ire
because, by its very nature, complaining narrows your
view so you can't see the way out. Instead of a solution,
you look for validation that your misery is justifiable. To
avoid the trap of groveling instead of getting better,
express gratitude as much as possible.

If you're unaccustomed to expressing gratitude, get
some practice. Put yourself on a regimen of no fewer than
three expressions of gratitude a day to get back in shape.

Express gratitude twice as often as you complain to
leave the world a better place than you found it.

> *Whining is not only graceless, but can be dangerous. It can alert a brute that a victim is in the neighborhood.*
>
> —MAYA ANGELOU

MAKE YOURSELF A MAGNET

A GRACIOUS RECEIVER KNOWS that the world is constantly offering her gifts—large and small—and she is grateful for all of them.

If you think there's nothing coming your way, you simply haven't developed your gratitude muscles. The more you moan about what you don't have, the less room there is for something wonderful to come along. You've trapped yourself.

That's what Caroline did at her fiftieth birthday party. Three of her four grown children attended the party and brought gifts. However, Caroline was inconsolable because her son David didn't come. She sighed and looked wistfully around the room during the party and said things like "I just wish David were here" and "I'm just so sorry David couldn't come." Instead of enjoying the company and affections of the three children who were there, she focused her energy on what she didn't have.

Caroline's husband and children were irritated and dejected that she didn't seem to appreciate their being there, and she missed connecting with them on her birthday. That's the danger of complaining about what you don't have. And since the rest of her family couldn't force David to attend his mother's gathering, Caroline was just spreading her own helpless feeling around the room to her husband and children, who ended up feeling that they hadn't done enough. Naturally, they could control only themselves—but that was lost on Caroline.

Of course, it's human nature to want to wallow in self-pity at times. That's because there's a perverse comfort in feeling sorry for yourself. Sometimes I'd rather focus on how everything is terrible so I can solicit sympathy or stay in bed or justify my mistakes. When I'm wallowing in my misery I don't even notice—much less receive—the gifts that are coming my way because I'm too preoccupied lamenting, just like Caroline. On some level, I *want* them to go wrong so I can continue to complain. Then, at least, I don't have to change, which, as we all know, can often be uncomfortable or difficult.

The problem is that clinging to unhappiness tends to result in a mopey face, a whiney voice, and slumping posture, all of which signal others to stay away. That kind of body language doesn't encourage anyone to help you or give you something to delight you.

When you're focused on what you don't have, you can easily overlook blessings that aren't quite what you expected. But if you ask yourself, "What have I received today?" you'll notice that concern, affection, consideration, and other niceties are being bestowed on you all the time.

GRATITUDE GETS YOU FURTHER

M Y TENTH-GRADE ENGLISH TEACHER, Mrs. Carpenter, assigned the class to write letters to companies with whom we had either been very pleased or very unhappy. The point was to learn how powerful and persuasive written communication can be, but she taught us another lesson along the way.

Most of us were quick to think of things we thought were unfair, so we wrote gripe letters. We were all impressed when the Frito-Lay company sent several bags of their product to one kid who complained about his underfilled bag of corn chips.

But Mrs. Carpenter insisted that for every negative letter we had to write *two* letters of gratitude to companies that had done something to please us. She told us that it was our duty to put twice as much positive energy into the universe as negative energy.

We received even more impressive responses from the positive letters than from the negative ones. When we praised a company's products or services, we were showered with free samples, passes, upgrades, gifts, and personal letters in return. One of the most memorable responses was from a local restaurant, whose manager decided to give our whole class a pizza party after one girl wrote to him with gratitude for their great service.

Make a habit of showing gratitude twice as often as you complain. If you fire off an e-mail pointing out what a coworker did wrong, be sure to thank two others who worked late to get the job done or always show up with a can-do attitude.

Gina did that, and she noticed that she felt less stress at the office. Was it because the people she had thanked were acting friendlier or because she was less focused on all the problems and more aware of all the positive aspects of her work? Maybe it was because she started a chain reaction of appreciation within her department that, in a small but meaningful way, changed the culture of her work environment and made being there more pleasant.

The optimist proclaims that we live in the best of all possible worlds; and the pessimist fears this is true.

JAMES BRANCH CABELL, *THE SILVER STALLION*

GRATITUDE IS A GLASS THAT'S HALF FULL

SOME PEOPLE FEEL they're being dishonest when they express gratitude if they don't feel entirely grateful. But like love, gratitude is as much an action as a feeling. Often we don't feel the gratitude until after we've expressed it. That means it's necessary to say thanks for something that wasn't as much as you expected.

It can be tempting to complain when you feel the service you get is lacking. I once hired a handyman to hang new doors in an apartment that John and I were preparing to rent. I had estimated that two days was plenty of time to complete the work, so I scheduled floor repair work for the third day. The handyman, however, didn't finish in the time I had allotted. I had to reschedule the floor repair, which was a headache.

When the handyman was done, I thanked him for doing a good job. A friend overheard me and asked, "How can you say he did a good job when he took so long to do something so simple and it put you behind schedule?"

I really *was* grateful for the handyman's quality work. True, he didn't finish within the time period that I hoped he would, but he charged a fair price to improve the apartment in a way that we couldn't. I wanted to trust that he was doing the best that he could, so I gave him the benefit of the doubt. I could have let him know that he took too long, but what would that have accomplished? It wouldn't have made him work a day faster, and even if it had, the quality of the work might have suffered.

So complaining had no upside. It would only have brought a sour note to the transaction, which resulted in quality work, and that was the most important thing to me.

As it was, my business deal with the handyman was pleasant, and the mission was accomplished.

The more I find the things I'm grateful for, the more full my glass gets.

My friend Lorraine had a similar experience regarding a home *she* was trying to rent. Lorraine hired a property manager to rent out her property for her. She signed a one-year contract at the beginning of the year, and later she discovered the manager was slow to return calls or make needed repairs on the property, but was quick to collect his fees whenever possible. When the year was up, Lorraine knew she didn't want to work with the property manager any longer. She called him and politely told him that she was planning to manage the property herself. She also thanked him for finding the tenants that occupied the home, and for keeping clear, accurate records. Granted, she could have complained about how unresponsive he had been, but she didn't because it wouldn't have served any useful purpose. She decided to leave things on a pleasant note.

The property manager responded by thanking her for her business, and he went on to make a few suggestions about how to make her new job of managing the property easier. He gave her the name of a software package that created those accurate records for which she thanked him. Lorraine ended up buying the software, and it did indeed make her job easier.

If she had decided to complain about the poor service she'd gotten over the year, chances are slim that the property manager would have wanted to help Lorraine. As it was, her gratitude made it easy for him to give her a helpful tip.

Joy is what happens to us when we allow ourselves to recognize how good things really are.

—MARIANNE WILLIAMSON

THE OPPOSITE OF GRATITUDE IS ENTITLEMENT

SOME PEOPLE CONFUSE GOOD RECEIVING with a sense of entitlement—when you start to take gifts for granted, or worse, act as if they're owed to you.

Marta exhibited this attitude recently when she tried to borrow Brenda's car and Brenda refused. Brenda had been letting Marta use her car on and off for weeks, so Marta took it for granted that she could use the car when she wanted. The first time Brenda exercised her right *not* to lend Marta the car, Marta was indignant. She was annoyed at Brenda's changing her mind when she assumed that she would have access to the car. Instead of thanking her friend for all the times she'd used the car, she was disappointed and angry. That's entitlement.

It's easy to see how Marta was being unreasonable in this situation, but most people don't recognize entitlement in themselves.

Catherine told me about how her mother, Evelyn, harbored a sense of entitlement that drove her whole family crazy. Catherine's able-bodied mother believed her grown children should help her maintain her home and do errands, and she told them this. This woman did say "thank you" every time her son fixed a leaky faucet or Catherine took her to the doctor, but she also tossed in a complaint. "Why don't you do this more often? How come I never see you?" These questions reflected her true feelings about these gifts: that she had a right to them. As a result, her gratitude sounded hollow—just as receiving a gift that you asked for is hollow. Catherine and her siblings were uninspired to do anything more for their mother, who seemed impossible to please.

Evelyn's children perceived her as a pit of need—one that her family could never hope to fill. Even if they wanted to help her paint the picket fence around her yard, they had to have the energy for both the painting and the barrage of complaints that would come afterward—without the benefit of seeing her satisfied and appreciative of their efforts. Evelyn could not be pleased, and no one wants to go near someone like that—let alone help her or give her presents.

One way to ensure that you don't develop a sense of entitlement is always to be pleasantly surprised by gifts or help—even when you're expecting them. Remember to marvel at them because they are always the result of someone else's generosity. Never assume that you should have them and, no matter what, don't complain. Instead of griping, count your long list of blessings.

GRATITUDE SHOWS THAT YOU'RE PLEASABLE

REMEMBER AS A CHILD when you'd opened all your presents on your birthday and you were still looking for more? Kids are like that. I remember complaining to my mom one

Christmas when I had just hit adolescence that I hardly got anything. I'd gotten a stereo, some clothes, books, a board game, and three records—not a bad haul. But I dismissed it all and whined that I didn't get anything because I was expecting much more.

Sure, I'd gotten some nice stuff, but even a whole store full of toys and clothes wrapped and put under the tree just for me wouldn't have helped because I wasn't pleasable at that time. I was experiencing teenage angst and had pinned my hopes on Christmas to cure me of it. I was looking for gifts that don't come in a box: contentment and freedom from self-consciousness. I didn't know that only I could give those things to myself, and I certainly hadn't learned to be gracious or grateful yet.

I was looking for something external—presents, in this case—to make me feel better, but what I really needed was something I could only get from myself: a better attitude.

Now that I'm well past adolescence, I still sometimes do the same thing: look to cure an internal problem with something outside of myself. Fortunately, I now realize that's what I'm doing as soon as I hear myself moaning and complaining. Once I recognize that I've become needy, I can try to figure out why that is, then give myself the thing I'm needing—whether it's to let go of something negative in my head or to go take a nap. I know I've succeeded when I'm back to expressing gratitude again.

A grateful woman expresses surprise and delight when she receives gifts because she doesn't assume that anyone should give her anything. When others see her delight, she is attracting more blessings because who, after all, doesn't want to bestow delight? When I have the opportunity to do something fun and spontaneous for someone I know will enjoy it and be happy, I do so because I love the warm feeling of pleasing someone else—especially when she least expects it. If you're brooding, moody, or unpredictable when receiving a gift or compliment, I'm less likely to keep trying to please you.

Intimacy is a difficult art.

—VIRGINIA WOOLF

GRATEFUL WOMEN HAVE BETTER ROMANTIC RELATIONSHIPS

RECEIVING GRACIOUSLY IS especially critical in romantic relationships because men, more than anything, want to please the women in their lives. If they're continually unsuccessful, they grow frustrated and the whole relationship suffers. They say things like, "No matter what I do, it just doesn't make her happy, so I've just about given up trying." One man who felt this way told me how he cleaned the whole house from top to bottom while his wife was away for the weekend, but when she came home she said, "It's wonderful except that you didn't dust. Do you see this dust?" She looked past the vacuumed floors, clean bathrooms, and sparkling kitchen to the bookshelves that he had missed.

That woman missed a chance to have a great connection with her husband. All she had to do was show that she appreciated his effort to please her. They could have basked in the warm glow that results when a man is chivalrous to a woman and she expresses her gratitude. Instead, they spent the rest of the day in their separate corners, feeling all the more distant for that exchange.

The intimacy they lacked was all for lack of gratitude.

Chapter 17

※

MARVEL AT SMALL THINGS

You don't have to wait for someone to give you a gift or to do something unexpected before you tell her you're grateful. You can thank the coworker who made a fresh pot of coffee, the spouse who emptied the dishwasher, the landlord who keeps your apartment well maintained. Expressing gratitude signals to others that you can tolerate good things.

Your positive attitude will create a culture of gratitude, and that will foster a pleasant connection to those around you—from the clerk at the dry cleaner whom you see every Saturday to those closest to you. You'll also be creating good karma that follows you in unexpected ways—like a stranger giving you his leftover tickets at the fair or finding a parking meter that's already paid up for the next hour.

> *The art of acceptance is the art of making someone who has just done you a small favor wish that they might have done you a greater one.*
>
> —Russell Lynes

Wake Up to Your Good Fortune

When Paula's romantic relationship was deteriorating, she was tempted to feel sorry for herself, but instead she decided to practice receiving as much as possible. When no one offered her a new pair of earrings or asked to take her out to dinner, at first she thought there was nothing to receive. But slowly she noticed her girlfriends were giving her extra hugs for support, her boss waited by his car so they could walk in together, and her teenage daughter paused long enough to ask gently and tenderly how she was. All were small gestures, but she was grateful for the little boosts she received throughout the day, and for the sense that she was cared for and loved—especially when she was struggling to feel that way.

Paula was still sad about her loss, but when she heard herself saying "thanks," she realized she was receiving some blessings after all. Instead of feeling abandoned, she knew she was loved.

That's exactly what gratitude does—it wakes us up to abundance and good fortune. That in turn makes us feel more cheerful and optimistic, which attracts more good fortune to us. That's because no one wants to exert effort trying to please someone who's wallowing in doom and gloom. Their efforts would be futile, for one thing, and who wants to risk offering kindness if it's going to be rejected? And since gloom can be contagious, others aren't likely to want to hang around a doomsayer.

All of us like to feel purposeful and know that we've contributed. Expressing our gratitude lets others know that they've done something.

That's great receiving.

Gratitude is not only the greatest of virtues, but the parent of all others.

—CICERO

SAYING THANKS WON'T MAKE SOMEONE STOP GIVING

SOMETIMES WE RESIST saying "thanks" because we have the false idea that the other person might stop doing the thing we appreciate. For instance, Cindy was afraid to thank her daughter, June, for doing the dishes after dinner because she feared the daughter would see her chore as optional. "It's taken me all this time to get her to do the dishes," she lamented. "If I thank her for doing her job, I'll have to start all over with teaching her that it's her responsibility."

Everyone likes to be appreciated for her work, even when she knows she's just doing her job. Imagine yourself in the same position—if your boss thanked you for meeting a deadline, you wouldn't assume that meant you could let the next one slide. If your daughter thanked you for making her lunch, you wouldn't take that as your cue to stop preparing food for her. You would, however, probably feel more cheerful and satisfied knowing that you're appreciated. In fact, you might be inspired to do these jobs with enthusiasm.

Cindy agreed that since she liked to be appreciated for carrying out her responsibilities, June would probably also enjoy some appreciation for doing the dishes. She also realized that saying "thanks" would help reinforce her daughter's likelihood of doing the dishes—not undermine it. So she decided to tell her daughter that she was grateful for her help in the kitchen.

In typical teenage fashion, June responded with a big smile—then by rolling her eyes and saying, "Whatever, Mom!" And when it was time to do the dishes the next night, she jumped right in. June seemed more willing than ever to take on the task that her mother was afraid she would abandon if she showed appreciation.

The greatest discovery of my generation is that human beings can alter their lives by altering their attitudes of mind.

—WILLIAM JAMES

BE GRATEFUL FOR THE THINGS YOU HATE

THE TRICK WITH GRATITUDE is to express thanks for everything just as it is, even if you don't feel grateful for your situation or think it should be different.

Naturally, there is plenty in life that you won't feel grateful for. Gratitude is not likely to be your first reaction to being stuck in traffic when you're in a hurry, starting to feel ill, or losing money. But when you curse your luck, you make yourself a victim because you take on the lopsided view that your situation is terrible.

Telling yourself that you're downtrodden is as good as making it so.

Sure some things are painful to endure, and you'd rather they didn't happen. Having gratitude will remind you that you always have a choice about what attitude to take.

Empowerment comes not from complaining but rather from embracing even that which displeases you.

A big part of finding that power is having connections with friends who can help point the way. Gratitude and good receiving help create and maintain those kinds of connections, and provide the space for those people to come into and stay in your life.

Sometimes it's hard to tell immediately whether you've been blessed or cursed by a turn of events, so a wise woman is grateful for everything. I went to a lecture where a woman told the following parable:

One day the only son of a rich farmer was plowing when the oxen got spooked and took off like a shot. The son tried to hang on to the plow and broke his leg. People in the town came by the farm to give their condolences. They told the farmer, "That's such bad luck about your son breaking his leg right in the middle of plowing season!" The farmer responded with a smile and said, "I'm thankful for everything just the way it is."

The following week, a war broke out. The army came by and drafted all the able-bodied young men for fighting. They passed over the farmer's son because he was injured. This time the townspeople said, "It's such a blessing that your son was hurt so the army didn't take him." The farmer responded the same way as before, "I'm thankful for everything just the way it is."

The farmer did well that next season, and he decided to use his bounty to add on to his already impressive house. When the people from the town saw the lavish house, they said, "You are very lucky to be the richest man in this town." Again, the farmer gave his usual response, "I'm thankful for everything just the way it is."

One day the farmer's son was playing poker when he ran out of money and decided to wager his family's farm. He lost, and the farmer and his family were forced to move out of their home. People thought this was very bad luck, and they told him so. Of course, the farmer said what he always said, "I'm thankful for everything just the way it is."

The following week the war finally ended, and the army came through and killed the wealthiest families and torched their houses as revenge for all the years of oppression by the rich. The farmer and his family, having only modest means at that time, were spared. The farmer repeated his mantra: "I'm thankful for everything just the way it is."

If you're like me, you might think that when something awful happens, you don't have to be grateful. However, since you don't yet know the final outcome, it can't hurt to be grateful for things exactly as they are; that is key to being a good receiver. This may sound impossible, and you are probably thinking, Well, how could someone who lost a parent or a child be grateful? That sounds perverse.

Granted, no one would ever be happy about a tragic event. It's normal to mourn a loss and even be angry about it. But that doesn't mean you can't still see the beauty around you.

WHEN LIFE THROWS YOU A HARDBALL, BE GLAD YOU'RE IN THE GAME

WHEN MY YOUNGER brother overdosed on drugs and alcohol and put himself in a coma, I felt a terrible loss. Where I once enjoyed the company of a sharp, witty young man with whom I thought I had so much in common, as of this writing he is capable only of blinking and breathing. I grieved to learn he had hidden so much of his pain from me.

In the weeks following my brother's tragedy, my sisters and I played a game we called Why My Life Sucks Since My Brother Overdosed. Our list included things like constantly feeling as if we'd been kicked in the stomach, being left without him to prepare for the upcoming birth of his first child, and having to deal with his medical insurance company. Not much gratitude there, I can assure you.

My feelings of frustration were human, of course, but they certainly didn't help improve my situation. My complaining was making me into a victim. From my point of view, his tragedy was happening to me and ruining my life. I had no control whatsoever over the situation, and I was angry because it hurt like hell and kept me from enjoying anything.

Not wanting to be a victim, I called my best friend to ask what it was I was grateful for in this situation, hoping she would know.

She reminded me that while I didn't *feel* gratitude for my painful situation, I would probably find more peace if I *chose* gratitude.

"Fine," I said, "I'm grateful that my brother overdosed on drugs. That's it—I'm really grateful." My words were hollow and sarcastic, but because of the magic of gratitude, I discovered something as I heard myself saying them.

"Wait a minute—I know what I'm grateful for. I'm grateful that I have a brother. I love him and his amazing mind. I love his sly sense of humor and his unorthodox views. I'm grateful that we spent so much time together and had such a great affection for each other. I'm grateful to have had a life-long friendship with someone who has the same coloring as me and who could laugh with me about our parents' idiosyncrasies. I'm grateful that he challenged my ideas."

The pain was the flip side of the joy that I'd experienced for all the years that I've known him.

I wouldn't trade the pleasure of knowing my brother for anything—even though it causes me incredible heartbreak now. I was not the victim of a tragedy but the *recipient of an amazing gift*. I didn't feel that way, however, until I changed my perspective by choosing gratitude. The root of my pain was not having the gift anymore. I compare it to watching a wonderful stage play and then crying and feeling like a victim at the end because the show is over. My relationship with my brother was much deeper and more significant than an evening's entertainment, but like a great play he has enriched my life—not ruined it. If I hadn't chosen gratitude, I might have overlooked the fact that I had received a gift at all.

Naturally, I feel grief and loss. But I can take the farmer's wise approach by saying to myself as much as possible, "I'm grateful for everything just the way it is."

When in doubt, give thanks.

Chapter 18

REJECT WHAT DOESN'T FIT FOR YOU

There are times when it's important to reject a gift, compliment, or help. If receiving something will cause you emotional or physical distress, or if it will keep you stuck in a situation that's unfulfilling and prevent you from having something better, then say, "No, thank you." If your instincts tell you that receiving from someone is unsafe, then listen to yourself and reject what's being offered. Otherwise, receive graciously.

Although rejecting what is offered is often hurtful to the person who wants to give you something, you can still maintain intimacy with that person by smiling, receiving the kindness, and being honest about why the gift doesn't fit for you.

It's more powerful to say no than it is to say yes.

—TOM HANKS

KNOW WHEN TO SAY NO

OF COURSE NOT EVERY GIFT that comes your way is going to be right for you. A friend might offer you her old dining room set that you hate, or invite you to a party where you know a lot of rowdy people will be drinking heavily, which will make you uncomfortable. Sometimes you will have to reject a gift—but you can still be gracious about it.

Wait a minute—didn't you say that I should graciously receive gifts, help, and anything else that comes my way?

I did say that, but I'm making an important exception here. If receiving the gift will *cause you distress,* then say, "No, thanks."

For instance, accepting a dining room set you don't want would cause you harm because it's not easy to move it, which is what you'd have to do to get rid of it after you receive it. That would set you back—not make your life easier. If someone wants you to come to a party where everyone else will be drinking heavily and you'll feel pressured to drink a lot, too, you can't attend without suffering emotional distress. In each of those instances, it's appropriate to reject what's being offered.

On the other hand, if someone gives you a scarf and you hate scarves, there's no harm receiving it graciously and finding something nice to say about the scarf or the giver, such as, "What a gorgeous color," or "You are so thoughtful," and of course, "Thank you." In that case you might as well receive the thoughtfulness, since you can easily pass the scarf on to someone who will enjoy it.

See the difference?

Receiving the scarf doesn't help you, but it doesn't hurt you either. And receiving the thoughtfulness will make you both feel good.

As long as it doesn't cost you time, energy, or heartache to receive a gift, then go ahead and take it as a way of fostering intimacy and staying in good receiving practice, especially if the gift is from someone dear to you.

❧

You might argue that politeness isn't necessary with those to whom you are close. You could argue that your husband will understand if you tell him that you would prefer a painting instead of a necklace for your birthday, and that your girlfriend knows you well so it won't matter to her if you ask where she bought your gift so that you can exchange it.

True, loved ones are often the most forgiving and understanding people in our lives, but they deserve the same diplomacy and grace that you would offer to a casual acquaintance. You may feel dishonest when you find something nice to say about a scarf that you simply don't want, but really you're being mature and polite—and tactful. Graciousness is *most* important with people to whom you are most close because it helps maintain the feeling of safety that intimacy needs to thrive.

Regardless of how well you know someone, rejection is rejection. It always stings. Granted, your lover and friends will know that you're not rejecting them personally, but there is nothing as wonderful as being thanked and adored for a gift, for feeling that you have given the right gift or the right advice at the right time.

A gift you hate at first could become something you love. The people in your life stretch your horizons and expose you to new things. When someone with whom you have a very intimate relationship—such as a lover or an old friend—gives you a gift, you might consider *keeping* items that you're not crazy about at first. If they think the scarf they bought is a great color for you, don't be too quick to put it in the thrift shop bag. A good receiver is open to the possibilities that something she wouldn't have picked herself could enhance her life in unexpected ways.

Trusting your intuition means tuning in as deeply as you can to the energy you feel, following that energy moment to moment, trusting that it will lead you where you want to go and bring you everything you desire.

—SHAKTI GAWAIN

USE THE DISTRESS TEST

THE CRITICAL DISTINCTION between being a poor receiver and rejecting something that will cause you distress is that you make a *conscious decision* to reject the offer, rather than rejecting it as a knee-jerk reaction out of guilt or modesty. For instance, Kate's friend Sarah wanted to help out at Kate's wedding, which was in another city. "I could rent a car," Sarah offered, "so I could be available to run any errands." Kate knew that Sarah didn't have much money, so she said, "Thank you for the offer, but really, I don't want you to spend money on renting a car." However, since Sarah offered, Kate missed a chance to receive and instead reacted out of guilt that her friend couldn't afford what she was offering. That's not rejecting something that doesn't fit— that's poor receiving.

Next, Sarah said, "If anything comes up, I can always borrow your car and help with errands that way." This time, Kate reacted out of a different emotion: fear for her car's safety. She knew Sarah to be a distracted driver who was always getting into fender benders. When she said, "Thanks a million for offering, Sarah. So far, I think we're okay," Kate was rejecting the offer out of her sense that it might do her harm to receive Sarah's kindhearted offer. That's not poor receiving—that's rejecting something that's distressing.

REJECT THINGS THAT GET ON YOUR VERY LAST NERVE

REJECTING OFFERS THAT WILL CAUSE you psychological harm is just as important as rejecting offers that will cause you physical harm. Donna learned this after accepting Stephanie's invitation to go for a walk after work. Donna was looking forward to the walk, knowing that it would feel good to stretch and breathe the fresh air on a beautiful spring day. However, when Stephanie spent the entire walk complaining about her mother, her boss, and her ex-husband, Donna ended up feeling like the dumping ground for Stephanie's grievances. When she arrived home, she felt worn down—not revived and full of endorphins, which is what she had hoped a walk with Stephanie would bring.

The next time Stephanie called to offer to walk together, Donna politely declined. She knew that listening to all that negativity would wear her down psychologically and cancel out the high she would normally get from taking a long walk.

The world stands aside to let anyone pass who knows where he is going.

— David Starr Jordan

Good Things Come to Those Who Say, "No, Thanks."

Another valid reason to reject a gift is if receiving it will keep you stuck in a situation that's unfulfilling.

My friend Richard had been a Realtor for years, but he found he didn't have the temperament for it and began dreading his work. Finally, one day, he decided that he was resigning from real estate for good, even though he didn't know exactly what he was going to do instead. He announced his decision to his friends and family with some trepidation.

A few days later, he ran into an old client who said she had recommended Richard to a neighbor who wanted to sell her house. Richard smiled warmly and said, "Thank you so much for thinking of me. I'm flattered that you would recommend me. Unfortunately, I won't be able to help your neighbor sell her house because I'm no longer working in real estate. However, I have an associate who's terrific, and I'll have him call your neighbor."

Richard could not accept the gift his client was offering— a referral for business he didn't want—because doing so would have put him right back in the career that he was trying to leave, delaying his pursuit of his new goal. He *did* receive her kindness, which is just as good in terms of creating a pleasant exchange and connection. He even managed to salvage the referral for an associate who gave him a finder's fee.

Shortly after that, Richard received an offer to head up a small nonprofit organization, which he accepted and found much more satisfying than selling real estate. Had he taken the referral, he would have been mired in the same unsatisfying work he had been trying to get out of. "It was very tempting to take that listing, since it was right in front of me, but something about saying no to the work that didn't fit for me seemed to make space for the work that does," Richard told me.

Richard had discovered the power in saying, "This is not for me." If we fill up with things that are unsatisfying, there's no room for the good stuff to come in. It's like eating junk food at your desk all morning and then having no appetite for the beautiful catered lunch. That's why it's so important to reject things that will keep you stuck.

Tammy learned this when she had a long-distance romance with Ted. She had hopes that they would eventually be able to live closer, but the signals didn't point to a future together. Although Ted called almost every day, he rarely made plans to see her. Sadly, Tammy knew that there was no future in this romance, and she decided to end it. Alarmed at the prospect of losing Tammy, Ted quickly offered to take her on a ski trip. Tammy knew that the ski trip would be a pleasant distraction from the real problem: that she was in a dead-end relationship that was never going to result in their being together in the long term. Tammy wanted a relationship that had a good chance of ending in marriage. She no longer wanted to foster intimacy or create a pleasant connection with Ted, a man whom she would not marry, so she responded by simply saying, "I'm sorry, but I can't go."

Rejecting the offer to go on a trip with Ted couldn't have been more appropriate for her happiness and sense of well-being. The day Tammy rejected Ted's offer to go on a ski trip was the day she started healing from the loss of that unsatisfying relationship. Saying no helped her create room in her life for a man who would cherish her and want to spend time with her. Rejecting Ted made it possible for her to start seeing Marco several months later. Marco absolutely adored and cherished Tammy and couldn't wait to spend time with her.

Nature abhors a vacuum and will try to fill it. In other words, keeping space open for the right person or thing is a powerful way to draw it to you.

A good receiver is constantly clearing out space in her life for the right things to come in by rejecting the old stuff that doesn't fit.

LISTEN TO YOUR SPIDEY SENSE

FEELING *unsafe* is an important reason to reject help or compliments. Even if all you have is a nebulous, nagging fear, do not put yourself at risk by receiving help or a gift from someone you mistrust. Heed your gut—the part of you that's warning you to be cautious. Not wanting to hurt someone's feelings is not a good reason to put yourself in danger.

In *The Gift of Fear* author Gavin de Becker talks about how a gnawing, uneasy feeling will always have a factual basis. For instance, a man who insists on giving you a ride when you've already said, "No, thanks," might set off alarms in your gut, even though on the surface it appears as if he's just trying to be a gentleman. Your gut may be telling you that this man doesn't take no for an answer, which means you certainly aren't safe with him.

De Becker says that every crime has a warning and that you can avoid victimization by trusting the phenomenon of "knowing without knowing why." De Becker writes that just before a crime, "there is a process as observable, and often as predictable, as water coming to a boil." If a man tries to give you something or take you somewhere and you see the equivalent of tiny bubbles forming and steam beginning to rise, soundly reject that offer. Trust that intuition.

Let's say a man you were interested in dating invited you to meet him at a hip, new club, and you wanted to attend but suspected it would be dangerous to go there by yourself late at night. You would either have to express your concerns and ask him to pick you up and escort you, or you would have to decline the offer altogether to protect your safety.

There's nothing wrong with letting your instinct tell you when to walk away. If that's what your gut is telling you, do it with confidence.

Chapter 19

❧

FOSTER ROMANCE WITH RECEIVING

When you receive from a man, you give him the gift of feeling masculine and purposeful. Receiving from the romantic lead in your life will contribute to greater intimacy and satisfaction in the relationship, and not receiving will cause frustration, tension, and friction.

You deserve special treatment and protection just because you're a woman. Recognize that the simple act of receiving graciously is an important contribution. You can inspire a man to greatness just by being a great receiver.

Sex is also a gift, so let your lover give you pleasure as much as he wants to. Lie back and let him explore every inch of your body. Remember that rejecting sex with your lover signals a rejection of the relationship.

I guess you're just what I needed. I needed someone to please.

—THE CARS

LET HIM PLEASE YOU

SINCE A BIG PART OF being feminine is receiving well, and what men are fundamentally attracted to is femininity, being a good receiver makes you more attractive to men. That's part of the way men and women are designed to go together— women enjoy being cared for and treated, while men have a complementary desire to provide and protect. Part of a man's nature is to want to provide for and please a woman.

Evelyn discovered this when she was making arrangements for a trip. Normally, she would have taken public transportation home from the airport, but this trip was going to put her on the Metro after dark. When she fretted about this out loud to her husband, he said, "Over the weekend, I'll drop off the car for you so you can drive home from the airport and I'll take the train home." Evelyn was tempted to say, "You don't need to take time out of your weekend to do that for me," but instead she decided to receive by saying, "You take such good care of me. I really appreciate your doing this." Her husband surprised her by saying, "It's the least I can do. You've been taking good care of me for fifteen years, and I don't tell you or show you often enough." Evelyn felt moved and delighted by his words. They grinned at each other for a few moments.

I picture this exchange—and the resulting connection—being like an electrical current that Evelyn's husband sent toward his wife, and that she received it in such a way that it made them both light up. Evelyn was glowing from feeling taken care of, and her husband was shining from being the one who had taken care of her. Giver and receiver were both lit up, as they had both been given something.

The warmth and emotional connection from those tender words lasted for days.

WHAT MAKES A MAN FEEL SUCCESSFUL

W HEN I WAS WRITING *The Surrendered Wife*, I asked hundreds of men how important it was to them that their wife or girlfriend be happy. They all said the same thing—"It's everything," "It's imperative," "It's *very* important," and even "If she's not happy, what's the point?"

I was astounded. I expected them to say that they liked making the women in their lives happy, but I didn't anticipate hearing that one of the most important things in their lives was to please their girlfriends and wives.

Their conviction and passion continue to amaze me.

My survey taught me that men of all ages and cultures take tremendous pride in pleasing a woman, and when she is happy they feel purposeful and successful. I also discovered that for many men, the alternative—providing only for themselves—seemed lonely and empty. They preferred to care for and protect a woman because it made them feel masculine.

Bob and Carol's situation is a good example. Bob drives in traffic nearly four hours a day to and from his job so that they can afford to live in a house in the country where Carol can see the stars at night. Bob doesn't seem to mind. He just wants Carol to be happy.

Ed feels the same way about Jan, which is why, when she wanted to see the very first showing of the new *Star Wars* movie, he got up at dawn to wait in line all day for tickets. Jan was thrilled, of course, which was all the reward Ed needed.

Jared was also happy to sacrifice for Bonnie when he moved two thousand miles away from his family to be near her family in the high desert of California. What did he get for that? Bonnie's gratitude, which was plenty for him.

I didn't realize growing up that I had something amazing and precious to offer the world with my feminine ability to receive. Instead, I got the distinct impression that I would be valuable only if I accomplished things—preferably professional, work-world things. I learned that women who had come before me had fought hard so my generation of women wouldn't have to depend on anyone. The message was clear: You can and should be self-sufficient. From an early age, I prized my ability to pull my own weight. But I put too much emphasis on independence. Instead of gaining inner strength from knowing I could be self-reliant, I sent out the smug, prickly message, "I don't need any help from anyone." No wonder I was lonely.

What I believed was a stark contrast to what I learned from the men I surveyed: They wanted to be intellectual and emotional equals with women, but they also desired the opportunity to *give* to them.

Want him to be more of a man? Try being more of a woman!

—Coty perfume ad

Rejecting His Offers Is Emasculating

I HAVE A HARD TIME convincing some women that men really want to please their wives and girlfriends. Many women tell me that their husbands or boyfriends never do anything to please them, or that their man is the exception. One woman described how her husband bought her car parts—for his car—for Christmas. However, these women had been such poor receivers for so long that their men had no idea how to please them. These women didn't realize that they had all but squelched their partners' efforts to delight them by rejecting them repeatedly.

For instance, Debra criticized her husband's birthday presents because they were never things that she would have picked out for herself. She routinely exchanged them for items she preferred. Over time, her husband grew weary of failing in his efforts to buy something that she would like and stopped trying. Debra then complained that he never even bought her a birthday present and that she felt hurt as a result.

At first, Debra didn't see how she had contributed to her own problem. Once she learned about the art of receiving graciously, and how important it is to a man to feel successful in making his wife happy, she felt terrible about her behavior from the past. Fortunately, it was relatively easy to correct. She started by apologizing to her husband, and she told him sincerely that she wished she had kept the things he had lovingly chosen for her. Her husband seemed relieved and soon after came home with flowers from the grocery store. They weren't the ones she would have picked, but they were beautiful and she told him so. It wasn't long before he was back to buying her full-fledged birthday presents and even no-special-occasion presents. Debra graciously received them all—and this time, she kept them.

Debra's husband probably felt much more successful about his ability to please his wife, which was very important to him (like most men). The intimacy and warmth in their relationship improved dramatically. Both Debra and her husband felt more loved because of this simple change.

There is a courtesy of the heart; it is allied to love. From it springs the purest courtesy in the outward behavior.

—JOHANN WOLFGANG VON GOETHE

CONSIDER KEEPING PRESENTS YOU HATE

O<small>F COURSE, KEEPING AND ENJOYING</small> the items that someone else picks out for you takes you out of control. He might buy the wrong color or size. He might choose a knickknack that isn't your style. Still, if the romantic lead in your life—who knows you well and loves you deeply—buys something because he thinks it will please you, consider keeping it.

Keep in mind that part of what he's attracted to is your receptivity—your femininity. Without that, you're difficult to please, which will make him feel emasculated because he is failing at his most important responsibility. That can easily discourage him from trying to please you in the future.

Wendy laughed when I made this suggestion because it called to mind a gift that she had rejected from her ex-husband years ago. "Ray had come home from work bursting with excitement to give me a present he'd bought out of a catalogue shortly after we were married," she told me. "It was a tan Naugahyde purse with my new initials—WAD—in large gold letters emblazoned on it. It was the ugliest thing, and it said 'WAD' on the side of it. I never carried it, and I remember he was crushed by my reaction."

We laughed a little, and I said, "Well, maybe that purse would never have grown on you, even if you'd used it every day," but Wendy shook her head. "I do wish I would have carried that purse. It would have meant so much to him, and it wasn't that big of a deal for me. Maybe I wouldn't be divorced from my daughter's father if I had," she said.

That may be a little extreme, but it is true that little things make a big contribution to the culture of a relationship. Perhaps using a Naugahyde purse would have made for a happier marriage for Wendy.

There is a woman at the beginning of all great things.

—Alphonse Marie Louis de Lamartine

You Won't Owe Him Anything in Return

Let's say a man offers to treat you to an expensive night out, but you worry that he can't afford it. You might be tempted to reject the offer for his sake—to save him money. You could tell yourself you're being considerate and sensitive, but really you're being controlling and mothering. You are signaling that you don't trust him to be able to take care of himself, so you're doing it for him.

Wouldn't you hate it if that were done to you?

Nothing could be more condescending, which is unattractive and off-putting.

Remember that a man who wants to take you out is not offering you steak and wine and good music so much as he is asking for the opportunity to connect with you. Dinner and a movie are just the vehicle for getting to know you better, making you laugh, and finding common ground. Rejecting his offer is rejecting the opportunity to connect with him.

If a man wants to treat you, it's not your responsibility to open his bank statement and decide if he can afford it. Your job is to look at it from your point of view. Would you like to go out to dinner and to a show? If you would, then go—and be sure to say "thanks." You're not taking something from him when you let him spend his money on you—you're giving him the gift of receiving, and allowing for the possibility of intimacy between the two of you.

If you're worried about his offer costing him too much, maybe the real problem is that you feel you're going to have to pay him back somehow. But nobody said you were going to owe him anything. So before you get all twisted up, try taking each gift in the moment.

When you see a guy reach for stars in the sky, you can bet that he's doing it for some doll.

—FRANK LOESSER, "GUYS AND DOLLS"

SEX IS A GIFT

AFTER SIXTEEN YEARS OF MARRIAGE, Holly was surprised when her husband suddenly made it his mission in life to explore every millimeter of her body and study exactly how to give her the utmost pleasure.

Uncomfortable with the intense scrutiny and vulnerability, Holly wished that he would focus on his own pleasure instead of just hers. Finally, she told him that she felt too self-conscious to enjoy herself when he was devoting so much energy and attention to her.

He responded by saying, "You don't have to be self-conscious with me! I'm your husband. I just want to make you feel good. So just relax and let me do that."

At that point Holly was forced to practice receiving sexually even though she wasn't totally comfortable with it. "Before, I was cheating myself out of something really wonderful, so that wasn't so great," she told me. "Now, I just try to practice relaxing and telling him what I like. What's so horrible about that? But for some reason, it makes me insecure. Everything hinges on my pleasure, and that's just a little intense for me."

As with all receiving, you have to be able to stand the awkwardness and the pleasure of being the center of attention when you're receiving sexual stimulation from a man.

Giving in to that discomfort will cause you to miss out. Even worse, rejecting your lover's sexual advances will put a chill on the intimacy every time. Allowing him to give you all the pleasure he wants will help you develop a higher tolerance for enjoyment. Think you can stand that?

Good! Because things really will get as good as you can stand.

Sex is as important as eating or drinking and we ought to allow the one appetite to be satisfied with as little restraint or false modesty as the other.

—Marquis de Sade

Rejecting Sex Is Rejecting the Relationship

WHEN MIMI TOLD HER HUSBAND that she was simply too busy to go away with him for the weekend, she couldn't understand why he seemed so miffed about it. She thought he'd be content to play golf with his buddies. It was one of the last nice weekends of the summer. When we were discussing it, it occurred to me that a weekend away would probably have included lots of time for lovemaking. Perhaps her husband heard her objections—that there was too much to do at home—as, "I don't want to be alone with you" or "I don't want to have sex with you." Those are hurtful words, and although she didn't say them, perhaps her husband was feeling the sting from that implication, which made it understandable that he was so bent out of shape.

Since sex is an opportunity for a man to give you pleasure, turning down your lover is rejecting a gift—and so much more. Rejecting sex with your husband is one of the worst things you can do for intimacy because in a way you're rejecting the relationship. Whatever the reason—you're too tired, you're not in the mood, you're too busy—the results are the same. You're passing up a physical and spiritual connection with the man you love.

When you hear yourself saying you're too tired to make love, check to see if there might be a deeper reason. It could be—and often is—that you're angry or resentful toward him and therefore may be withholding to make a point. If that's the case, then you've identified the problem that needs to be addressed. Make fixing that problem a priority so that you can start receiving passion and pleasure again. Then you can stop deepening the chasm that has opened up between you and him, which has likely made him feel dejected and frustrated.

The only thing that makes your romance different from every other relationship you have is that you have physical intimacy. Take that away, and you're left playing the part of roommates.

But if you find the courage to receive his efforts in bed, you'll both get to enjoy an amazing connection and outrageous pleasure.

Chapter 20

❧

LET A MAN SUPPORT YOU

If it's true that behind every great man is a woman, it's because she inspired him with her gratitude, respect, and receptivity—not because she put him through medical school.

Gratitude, respect, and receptivity are even more powerful than any financial contribution you can make toward your husband's success, and he can get those things only from the woman he loves and who loves him.

Instead of supporting the whole family, consider what you might be able to contribute by being receptive and grateful. Consider letting him support you.

There's no telling what you might inspire.

If women didn't exist, all the money in the world would have no meaning.

—ARISTOTLE ONASSIS

DON'T TRY THIS AT HOME

HAVE YOU EVER HEARD about the woman who put her husband through medical school only to have him leave her for another woman?

Of course you have, because this isn't an isolated incident: Putting a guy through medical school or law school or supporting him while he starts his business or for any other reason is stressful for the woman and emasculating for the man. Instead of being able to make his wife happy, the man in this predicament has to receive from her. He is powerless to do what his instincts tell him to do and what all men I've ever talked to say they want to do: provide for and please his wife.

A woman who supports a man is living on the edge. She is the one whose paycheck covers the mortgage, buys the food, provides some entertainment, and pays every other bill with their name on it, leaving the man little to give.

Such a woman may be tempted to control him and the household. She might try to curb his spending, since it's her sweat that's earning the money. She might want to oversee his studying habits, since she is footing the bill for his tuition.

She would begin to see her husband as a little boy who needs her supervision—which is just not a good basis for a healthy sex life and emotional closeness in the relationship.

Men, I know, want to please the women in their lives more than anything.

A man who feels that he cannot give anything to his wife or girlfriend will be desperate to find a woman he *can* please. The wife would be desperate to find someone who will take care of her and treat her instead of the other way around. The setup here is terrible: Everyone gets bent out of shape because nobody is playing to their strengths as a man or a woman.

The point is that men love to please women. If you aren't in a position to be pleased, they will move on or be frustrated.

If there hadn't been women we'd still be squatting in a cave eating raw meat, because we made civilization in order to impress our girlfriends.

—ORSON WELLES

LET A GOOD GUY SUPPORT YOU

I KNOW IT'S NOT POLITICALLY CORRECT to say so, but women want a man to cherish, adore, and protect them, and men feel a complementary drive to provide because it's an expression of masculinity. Therefore, consider letting a man support you through the transition from work you hate to work you love—or letting a man support you, period.

Of course, you can't take this plunge unless you trust that he is going to take care of you. If you're wondering if you can trust your man, first ask yourself if you have a good guy. As long as your guy is capable of being faithful to you, is not an active addict, and is not physically abusive, then you have a good man and you can relax into his care without fear that he will leave you high and dry.

The next question you might be asking yourself is, "Will he start to resent me?" As with all gifts, remember that gratitude is key and that a sense of entitlement is always unattractive. If you begin to feel that he should support you and you forget that it's a gift, that could certainly cause resentment. As long as you keep your perspective, you'll both enjoy the intimacy from the exchange of your trust and faith for his care and support.

Of course, you can always wreck it by becoming resentful. Rhonda explained that while she was grateful that her husband's income enabled her to leave her job and stay home with their children, which had always been her dream, she sometimes felt she owed him something. She would try to be a superwoman by making an elaborate dinner and cleaning out the garage to try to repay him. As a result, she felt that she wasn't spending her time doing what she really wanted to do—and she was tired and bored, which led to feeling resentful toward him, as if he were forcing her to cook and clean, even though he hadn't asked for anything. From there she would flip into feeling as if she was *entitled* to having his financial support since she worked so hard to make sure he had clean underwear every day.

Meanwhile, her husband kept working and kept paying the bills. After having lunch with a friend who worked full time and had two small children, Rhonda was reminded about how fortunate she was to have her husband supporting her. She remembered that he was giving her the gift of being able to be home with her children.

If either one of you starts to become resentful, remember that financial support is a gift, and when you receive such a gift the only gracious response is gratitude.

Behind Every Great Man Is a Very Surprised Mother-in-Law

BIANCA MARRIED FOR THE FIRST TIME in her early thirties, so she was accustomed to supporting herself. Since she and her husband, Craig, had debt from the wedding and the honeymoon, she felt it was important that she continue to work to pay down the debt, even though she was exhausted and unhappy with her job. Craig invited her to quit working several times, but she refused because she was worried about what his mother would think. "I didn't want her to think I married her son as a meal ticket," she said. But Craig kept insisting that he made enough to support them both and that they could pay the debt back a little at a time.

One night a friend was having dinner at their home when Craig said that he hated to see Bianca so unhappy and working so hard. He wished she would just take some time off for herself. Bianca's friend said, "That is so sweet that your husband wants to support you! Why don't you let him?"

That's when Bianca finally realized that she had been rejecting her husband's offer.

Because they didn't have kids, Bianca felt entirely undeserving of the financial support that Craig provided. But as she settled in and began to relax, Craig kept saying how pleased he was to see her happy and rested when he came home. "That seemed to mean a lot to him," Bianca reported, "and it's been a wonderful gift for me. I know I'll go back to work someday, but for now, the best thing I can do for me—and for our marriage—is to think about what job will give me pleasure and enable me to be a pleasant, rested, and happy person. Why should Craig have to be around someone who is tired and frustrated all the time? That's how work was making me feel.

"We still have debts, but I feel I'm improving our quality of life as a family. Plus, I feel like the queen knowing that I don't have to work. I still feel like I'm getting away with something amazing."

Queens have pretty good self-esteem, so it's easy to see how Bianca's good receiving skills helped increase her confidence. And Craig felt proud that he could take care of his wife so well.

YOU'RE HIS INSPIRATION

---·ᴄⱱ꜀·---

THE SIMPLE ACT OF RECEIVING gives a man a chance to feel good. It creates a pleasant connection between the giver and the recipient. Letting your man pay your way for a bit requires both the humility of admitting you could use help and the self-esteem to know that you're worth helping. It allows a man to feel strong and appreciated.

Women who rely on their husbands for financial support to stay home are one example of this combination of humility and self-esteem. Such a woman bestows tremendous trust in her husband, and often inspires him to go higher than he ever imagined he would before she put the responsibility squarely on his shoulders with complete faith that he would rise to the occasion.

Sheila told her husband, Brandon, that she wanted to stay home with their son. Brandon was willing to support his family, but he was terrified because his real estate appraisal business earned only about half of Sheila's executive salary. Sheila was willing to scale back and rely on Brandon's income so that she could make raising their son her priority.

Brandon felt a fierce motivation to meet the challenge of supporting his family. Within a year, he had doubled his income, and in three years he was making more than their previous combined income.

Sheila's willingness to receive from Brandon inspired him to become more accomplished and successful and allowed her the freedom to stop working outside the home. If she had clung to the idea that she should be self-reliant and decided not to receive Brandon's financial support, she would have been denying herself the life she really wanted at home with her child, and taken on the stressful role of being a full-time working mom. Brandon would never have become as accomplished without her complete faith and knowledge of her desire, and their son would not have had the benefit of a stay-at-home mom. The whole family would have suffered if Sheila hadn't been willing to let Brandon support her. As it is, Brandon couldn't be prouder of taking care of his family.

Brandon was successful in increasing his earning to support the whole family partly because Sheila also relinquished control of how he did it. She hoped he would, but she didn't *expect* him to do any better than he was already doing. She didn't give him instructions on how to be more profitable, or tell him to hire some help or spend more on advertising. That kind of control would have undermined his self-esteem and made it difficult for him to trust himself, which is critical for running a successful business.

Letting go of how it happened or when it happened helped Sheila receive a wonderful gift from her husband.

Love cures people, both the ones who give it and the ones who receive it.

—DR. KARL MENNINGER

WHAT INSPIRES A MAN

IN CONTRAST TO INADVERTENTLY REJECTING presents from men, when we receive well and express our desires, women can inspire men to new heights. When you receive from a man, you give him someone to provide for and protect. You give him someone to please. That, in turn, makes him feel purposeful and strong.

An artist I know named Dina spent most of her time painting and made little money selling her art, but she lived comfortably because she also had a boyfriend who was happy to support her. Dina told me that her boyfriend wasn't earning much when they met, but that she inspired him to make more money so he could support them both and she could focus on her art. Suspicious, I asked her how she did that. At first, she said she wasn't sure, but as we spoke she told me, "Paul has always been so sweet to me. His job was pretty menial and he didn't have much, but he would make me dinner, help me put up blinds, and always be doing something thoughtful for me, so I appreciated that. Then after we were together for a while I noticed that he was an amazing photographer, so I would tell him I thought he was talented.

He said he wished he could support me, and I told him I would love that.

"Then he said he'd been thinking about becoming a professional photographer but didn't have a clear idea about how to do it. He was always talking about different ideas for starting a new career, but none of them struck me as particularly great ideas, so I wouldn't say much—until he said he wanted to be a wedding photographer. When he said that, I was all over it. I knew he would be great at that, and I told him so. He went out and started assisting other wedding photographers. Then he got his own studio, and two years later he was making six figures and was one of the best wedding photographers in the area. I always knew he would be a success."

Dina did four distinct things that seemed to contribute to Paul's success:

- **Gratitude:** Dina spoke in terms of gratitude about Paul. He was always doing something thoughtful, and she was appreciative.
- **Expressing her desire:** When he said he wanted to support her, she reacted with pleasure. She was happy already, but she let him know that if he supported her, that would make her even happier. Now, he had something to shoot for.
- **Mirroring:** Dina let him know that she saw his talent. When he came up with ideas, she helped him by showing her enthusiasm *only* when he came up with an idea that she thought was really great—otherwise, she didn't say anything. She *didn't* say, "That's not going to work,"

when he came up with a clunker. She just waited for him to come up with a better idea. That's a perfect example of positive mirroring.

- **Faith:** She told him she believed he would succeed. And so he did.

"He has to work almost every Saturday," Dina told me, "which I think is quite a sacrifice to make. I wouldn't want to have to do that. But I know he's doing it partly because he likes supporting me, which makes me even more grateful."

Perhaps knowing that Dina wasn't going to complain that he was gone every Saturday was also part of Paul's success. He didn't have to worry about his girlfriend saying, "You're never here on the weekends." Instead, she viewed his absence as part of a sacrifice he made for her benefit. In other words, it was all part of a gift she received graciously. Dina was willing to *receive* financial support from the man in her life, and because she was hoping for but not expecting him to do better, he rose to the occasion.

You might think Dina was only using her boyfriend for her own financial gain. However, since she had been attracted to and romantically involved with him when he wasn't earning much, she obviously wasn't just interested in his money. Her boyfriend certainly didn't feel used. He felt proud and masculine about his ability to support her with his newfound income.

I have come to believe that giving and receiving are really the same. Giving and receiving—not giving and taking.

—JOYCE GRENFELL

USE YOUR POWER WISELY

I ALSO KNOW WOMEN who have a *negative* impact on their romantic partners' earnings. For example Lillian complained that her husband—who was gainfully employed when she met him—was out of work and languishing while she was pregnant with twins. She also told me that two serious boyfriends she'd had before she met her husband were both out of work for most of the time that she had been with them.

"But they both went on to hold steady jobs with respectable pay after I broke up with them," Lillian admitted, "and the only thing those two guys had in common . . . was me."

Lillian's receiving skills were lacking. She was ungrateful for what she had and found fault with her husband's job. She unwittingly demeaned him by telling him what to do and treating him disrespectfully. Whatever the reason, Lillian probably didn't trust her husband to take care of her, and that made it nearly impossible for him to succeed.

You might think this is an extreme example, but it's not. Men glean their self-image from what they see in their wife-mirror. If she is grateful, receptive, and smiling, they see themselves as successful. If she is miserable, complaining, and demanding, they feel like failures.

What men see in the wife-mirror is then projected to the rest of the world. If the woman with whom he is closest doubts him, he starts to doubt his own capabilities. True, it might not make a man lose his job, but in Lillian's case, her husband suffered a layoff from which he had a tough time springing back because she had inadvertently chipped away at his self-esteem.

Your ability to receive from a man will also influence him for better or worse. If you graciously receive and appreciate what he's already giving you, and express the desire for things you still want without complaining, you give him the message that he is a success at his most important job: taking care of his woman. That's bound to have a positive impact on his self-esteem. If you are ungrateful or dissatisfied, you send the message that he's a failure, which will give him a negative opinion of himself.

Don't underestimate your power and influence in what he accomplishes. Use that power wisely by receiving and expressing gratitude.

THE MOTHER OF ALL RECEIVING CHALLENGES

IF YOU'RE ANYTHING LIKE I was and your receiving muscles are out of shape, you may have a very hard time depending on a man financially because it's the mother of all receiving challenges. However, if you do let him take care of you, you will be giving the romantic lead in your life an amazing gift, too: trust. There's no telling what that might influence him to do.

If you feel that you must accomplish and be productive, perhaps you don't recognize the value of femininity. Feeling that you don't have worth unless you accomplish is like thinking the flowers in the yard ought to do something to earn their keep. Just being a woman is valuable and important.

Chapter 21

✤

RECEIVE MONEY FOR WORK YOU LOVE

If you don't enjoy your work, explore the possibility of changing jobs—even if you think you could never get a better one than you have now. Use the principles of receiving—speaking your desires, accepting help, owning your gifts, and expressing gratitude—to bring better work into your life. Good receivers know what their gifts and talents are and are not afraid to say so or get paid for them.

> *Where our work is, there let our joy be.*
>
> —TERTULLIAN

MISERY MADE ME FEEL VIRTUOUS

WHEN YOUR WORK is making you unhappy, it's an indication that something is amiss and needs to change. Perhaps your work doesn't suit your talents and energy. Maybe the environment is no longer right for you. Maybe it's a fun job—for somebody else. Perhaps you're trying to force things that don't fit for you.

I particularly understand that last one because I'm always trying to force things that don't fit for me. I tried to work as a mortgage lender once for about a week before I ran out of the building screaming. I decided to be a software instructor on another occasion and actually garnered hate mail from a student—I was that bad. Another time I took a lucrative job writing an instruction manual on how to collect car payments from deadbeats, which depressed me. None of those jobs fit for me, and while that may seem pretty obvious, I really had no idea at the time.

That's because I thought having to work meant having to suffer.

I figured it didn't make much difference if I was dreading technical writing or teaching people how to use the newest version of PowerPoint because it was all a drag and always would be. Somehow, I got the message growing up that working for a living meant suffering. Perhaps it was because all the adults I knew hated their jobs and just did them because they had to pay the bills.

Activities that were once enjoyable became miserable as soon as I attached a salary to them. Remember that rock band I sang in? I thought it would be fun to sing and dance on stage in front of an audience with musicians behind me, playing the songs I wrote. And it was—until I made it unbearable. I did this by putting our band on a grueling rehearsal and perform-ance schedule. We played until we dropped and then started again. As depletion set in, tempers flared, we missed notes, and the whole point of doing something we loved for money was history.

Pushing the band relentlessly made it seem more serious to me, but it didn't make us any more successful. In fact, it caused the group's demise.

I secretly believed that we would succeed only if we were suffering.

To me, there wasn't any virtue in just having fun if radio stations everywhere weren't spinning our records. We couldn't just have fun and be playful and expect to be on radio stations everywhere. But the rest of the band was not interested in be-ing virtuous. They wanted to play because they loved to play, and when I made it tedious, they lost interest.

Unfortunately, I just didn't have a high tolerance for pleasure in my life at that time. I thought I was supposed to suffer a certain amount—especially if I was receiving money for the work—and the band helped provide my daily grind. That was what was comfortable and familiar to me. If I was going to take money for something, I had to suffer.

I told myself that sacrificing that way in the present would pay off in the future when we would succeed. *Then* we'd enjoy ourselves.

Your chances of success are directly proportional to the degree of pleasure you derive from what you do. If you are in a job you hate, face the fact squarely and get out.

—MICHAEL KORDA

IT PAYS TO PLAY

I WISH I HAD KNOWN THEN how to stand the enjoyment of playing in a band without making it drudgery. Not only would it have been more fun, we probably would have had more success, since a band that's enjoying itself is more inviting and has a better groove.

Some of the most highly paid people in the world make their living playing. They play music or baseball or basketball or tennis or chess. A wealthy real estate investor I know told me, "What I do is exactly like playing Monopoly." One study showed that the key difference between people who had achieved billionaire status and those who were (merely) millionaires was that billionaires *loved* what they did. In other words, financial success follows people who have a high tolerance for enjoying themselves while they work.

So what does this have to do with receiving? To love your work, you have to be willing to receive money for doing something that you enjoy. All of us have certain talents we're meant to share with the world. If you don't find work that uses those skills, you're rejecting your gifts instead of sharing them. When you bury your talents, you're blocking yourself from receiving. And staying in a job that doesn't appeal to you will block you from receiving the financial success, recognition, and satisfaction you deserve.

Becky is an example of a woman who buries her talents until after work hours. An administrative assistant from nine to five, she makes amazing handcrafted jewelry at night. Although her friends have told her how impressed they are with her talent and encouraged her to try to make it her living, she hasn't made a single move in that direction. Instead, she continues to work in a job she hates, which isn't suited to her creative talents. Only her friends know about the gorgeous jewelry she makes, and the world may never know what works of art she would create if she devoted her work life to doing what she loves. What a shame.

> Work is something made greater by ourselves and in turn that makes us greater.
>
> —Maya Angelou

Clinging to the Wrong Job Will Keep You from Getting the Right One

I KNEW A THERAPIST who saw a bunch of patients who were unhappy in their work. When she suggested to them that they consider changing jobs, they all said the same thing, "Oh, I could never make the kind of money I make now at another job. I was just lucky to get this position because my boss likes me. If I quit this job, I could never do as well."

After hearing from a half-dozen people who all thought they were overpaid in jobs they didn't enjoy but also thought they could never replace, the therapist came up with a plan. She joked that she was going to start a round-robin in which all of her unhappily employed clients would switch jobs with the next person to see if they liked the new position any better. "I wish I could demonstrate to everyone who thinks they have the only job like theirs in the world that there are plenty of others—maybe even one that's better suited to them."

Anytime you think something is irreplaceable, you will hold on to it very tightly. When you're clinging like that, there's no room to open your palms and receive something better. For instance, when someone else tells you about an opening or a training program, you may dismiss it instead of investigating it because you think you can never match the job that you have.

Holding something tightly blocks you from receiving something else because your fists are tightly shut around the object you value so much. But if that object—let's say a job—doesn't fit for you to begin with, it doesn't make much sense to hold on to it at all costs.

Yet I know a lot of women who do just that.

I've done it myself.

HOW RECEIVING CAN HELP YOU MAKE A CAREER CHANGE

So HOW DO YOU GET OUT of a job that doesn't fit without going broke or sinking into debt? As with everything else, an important part of receiving what you want in your work life is saying what you want—even if you can't be specific. Start by saying, at least to yourself, "I want a better job."

Since things will get as good as you can stand, consider expressing a more specific desire, like, "I want to dance in a Broadway musical" or "I want to quit my job and be a stay-at-home mom." I know this sounds like a small step, and it is, but you can't start to make a change without it. Now that you've loosened your stranglehold on the job that didn't fit for you, there's room for other opportunities to come into your life.

When it comes to talking about your current job, remember the power of gratitude. Say, "I've been so fortunate to have great coworkers and a generous compensation package," not, "If my boss weren't such a tyrant, maybe I wouldn't be trying to escape from that place."

Next, think about receiving help from people who love you. A friend of mine wanted to change jobs, but she couldn't get motivated to rewrite her résumé, even though her two-hour-a-day commute was crushing her spirit. I offered to write her résumé for her, but she declined. "I just have to get to it. There's nothing you can do," she told me. Perhaps she was right—it's tough to create a résumé for someone, but if she had agreed to have me come over to help, just knowing I was on my way would probably have motivated her to dust off the file. Having someone else there to bounce things off of never hurts. My friend still hasn't updated that résumé, and she's still making that brutal daily commute.

Even if no one is *offering* to write your résumé or introduce you to business contacts, you can ask for help or advice from people who have what you want. Most people are flattered when you ask them for advice. Just as when you are asking for advice about child care or relationships, the subtext of "Can I ask your advice about work?" is also "You seem to have it together in this area, and I admire your accomplishments and intelligence." Who wouldn't want to help someone who expresses admiration?

When love and skill work together, expect a masterpiece.

—JOHN RUSKIN

TELL EVERYONE ABOUT YOUR TALENTS

WHEN YOU DO TALK to other people about changing careers or just finding a better job, you'll want to own your gifts, even if you're not sure how they would fit into a new career. So instead of being modest about your accomplishments, be specific about how you've had only perfect performance reviews, made your department more efficient, motivated your team to exceed the sales goal, or created award-winning products. Even if you're not sure how it will apply to earning a living, you can tell everyone you know what a great eye you have for matching fabrics and furniture, how passionate you are about child development, or how well you manage a sailboat.

Cynthia wasn't sure what she wanted to do, but she knew that she had to get out of her stressful nursing job. She started by owning her gifts. She would say, "I'm a good listener, and my job is to listen to people and empower them." At first, she had no idea how that would help her put gas in the car and food on the table, but she clung to her intuitive sense that her ability and desire to listen well and empower others would play a part in her new career. She told everyone she knew about her ability and her conviction that it would play a big part in her next career.

One friend suggested that she look into becoming a personal coach, and Cynthia grew excited realizing that becoming a coach would require her to do lots of listening and empowering. Cynthia cut back on her hours at the hospital and experimented with how to make a career out of being a listener. At first, Cynthia offered her services for free to her friends so she could test the waters and get some experience. Today, she's a successful personal coach who listens to people's problems and then gently guides them toward change. Her clients are enthusiastic about her services, and they are happy to pay handsomely for them.

Cynthia couldn't have made that switch without owning her talents first.

Consider the idea that you, too, could be like Cynthia and make a great living doing what you love if you own your gifts, talents, and accomplishments.

To be surrounded by beautiful things has much influence upon the human creature: To make beautiful things has more.

—CHARLOTTE PERKINS GILMAN

IF YOU LOVE WHAT YOU DO, YOU'LL NEVER WORK A DAY IN YOUR LIFE

ANOTHER FORM OF OWNING your gifts is being willing to accept money when you use your talents for someone else's benefit. Money is one way that we acknowledge value, and when you refuse compensation for your talent you're saying that it isn't valuable.

One reason I used to do this is because I equated work with tedium and things like writing or singing with fun. If I wrote something, I figured I didn't deserve much money for it because it wasn't hard or unpleasant. I now realize it's okay to receive money for doing things that come easily. That's accepting payment for your gifts—and why not? Work doesn't have to be hard—it can be enjoyable. If you believe bumper stickers that say things like, "The worst day fishing is still better than the best day working," you might not think so. But my experience has been that things that pay very well can also be thoroughly enjoyable and even easy.

Linda had a job in landscaping, and a friend asked her how much she would charge to design a garden like the one she made for herself. She was tempted to say, "I'll do it for nothing if you pay for the plants and materials." She reasoned that since she loved gardening and she loved her friend, and she already had a job that paid the bills, she could give her services as a gift. But not wanting to undervalue herself, she decided to at least come up with what she thought her services were worth. She told her friend, "Normally, I'd charge $300 for the landscape design and another $800 for installation. But for you, I'll do it for $100 if you also make lasagna for dinner and help with the planting."

When someone asks you to do something that you're great at—even if it's not how you normally earn money—let her know how much value your gifts have by giving her a price. Later, if you decide to make a gift of your services, you can always do that—but first, establish the worth. Otherwise, the subtext of your message is, "My talent for gardening is nothing special or valuable." You dismiss your own gifts.

Of course, when someone offers to pay you for something that isn't what you normally get paid to do, you might not be sure how to respond. If you don't know off the top of your head, it's fine to say, "Let me think about it and get back to you."

When I'm determining my worth in the world, I prefer to give it some thought so that I don't mistakenly undervalue myself. The point is to accept money when you use your talents for someone else's benefit.

⚜

There's one more way that receiving will propel you forward at work: As you begin practicing receiving in every area of your life, your self-worth will improve from believing the compliments you hear. And, your financial worth will naturally follow as your confidence grows because other people will think you deserve more.

Chapter 22

✧

SPEAK FOR YOURSELF

Focus on your own needs and desires, instead of worrying about the people around you, and start receiving accordingly.

No matter how many times you forget to receive, you can always start again today—right now.

I'm not afraid of storms, for I'm learning how to sail my ship.

—LOUISA MAY ALCOTT

NOT EVERYONE WILL APPLAUD YOU

SYLVIA TOOK EIGHTEEN-YEAR-OLD Helen under her wing when Helen began working at the same company as an intern. Single and twelve years Helen's senior, Sylvia enjoyed guiding and mentoring Helen, and she even bought her a pair of shoes. She also paid for Helen's breakfast once, and for the movies another time. Helen responded by receiving graciously, which made giving her things all the more rewarding for Sylvia.

The problem? Helen's grandmother was full of criticism.

"You don't need to be accepting shoes or anything else from anyone outside of your family," she told the young woman. "You have a job now. Can't you pay for those things yourself?" The subtext of her grandmother's message was that Helen had done something disgraceful by accepting her coworker's generosity. The older woman's underlying fear was that her granddaughter was going to owe something. She wanted to keep Helen out of debt.

That's just one example of the crazy, mixed-up messages we may have gotten about receiving, so it's no wonder that many of us have a hard time with it. The beliefs and habits we have now came from somewhere, and it's usually not hard to trace them back to a well-meaning parent or grandparent who may have instilled in us a sense of shame about receiving.

However, those beliefs and habits aren't serving you anymore. Now that you know about receiving, you can change those habits to take advantage of all the pleasures that are offered for your enjoyment.

Just be aware that not everyone will applaud you. Others may see you as inappropriate or greedy. Some will feel uncomfortable as you change the culture of your relationships with them. Your friend who always argues over who should pay the bill may be surprised when you simply smile and receive her generosity. Your mother might be appalled that you don't keep track of whom you "owe" birthday presents to anymore. Even your husband or children might be irritated that you don't do as much for them as you used to. You may make some people very uncomfortable or jealous with your new approach, but that's not your concern, so don't let that stop you.

Your job is to focus on your own happiness, since that's the only thing you have control over anyway.

*Don't be afraid if things seem difficult in the beginning.
That's only the initial impression. The important thing is
not to retreat; you have to master yourself.*

—OLGA KORBUT

RECEIVING IS BETTER THAN THE ALTERNATIVE

ON THE LAST NIGHT of a four-week intimacy workshop I
had been teaching, everyone in our small group had bonded.
Women had forged new friendships, shared their deepest
secrets, and come to look forward to the intimate meetings.
We were all a little sad about the workshop's coming to an
end. I was surprised that many of the women had brought
me thank-you gifts—cards, books, candles, bubble bath, and
more. I was receiving everything graciously and gratefully,
and there was plenty to receive from my students, who spoke
passionately about how much they had gained from the
workshop and from me.

I was open and vulnerable with the women in my class, because that's the only way you can receive graciously. I had
been taking in amazing compliments and gratitude, as well as
thoughtful gifts. I was moved and grateful for the outpouring.

In some ways I was taking a risk by receiving that night.
After all, they were bringing me gifts that I may not have
deserved since they had paid for the workshop and I was just
doing my job. I accepted compliments at the risk of seeming

immodest in front of everyone, and, at the end, one person offered to help me put the chairs away, and someone else even offered to type a list containing everyone's e-mail address so the group could stay in touch. Everywhere I looked, someone was giving me something wonderful. I was in a professional situation, and I certainly didn't want anyone to think I was lazy or proud or greedy.

However, it felt wonderful to be the recipient of so much affection, and I was glad that I was able to take it all in. I also remember feeling a little uncomfortable, because I was clearly not in control. Rather, what I experienced was like being lifted up on their shoulders, which is a little precarious, but it also feels amazing. You're making yourself vulnerable when you're receiving, which can be a bit scary. That's what makes receiving harder than it sounds: You're taking a risk.

However, the alternative is to reject the kindness and sweet surprises that come your way so that you're never undefended. You'd have to be completely self-sufficient, do every tedious task yourself, and pass up the emotional connections you could be having with people who love you.

In my experience, receiving is a risk that's well worth taking.

❧

You may feel that time has already gone by that you could have been using to enjoy yourself, but it's never too late to start receiving. Even if you forgot to accept an apology this morning, or turned down help yesterday, you can start again right now.

A friend of mine said, "Learning to receive has made me feel like a princess. I was afraid that I would lose that feeling over time, but now I know that I can practice receiving any time, that it's always there for me. When I want to feel like the princess, I just have to find the willingness to be treated like one."

Now that receiving is a habit for me, the possibilities seem endless, and I find new delights each time I take on a new level of receiving. Being receptive has helped me become a happier wife, a more connected friend, and a more accomplished writer. I have more confidence, more time to relax, and a feeling that there is plenty in the world for me. I know that as I continue to receive, I'll be able to stand even more affection, prosperity, intimacy, and pleasure.

So will you—as soon as you start receiving graciously.

ABOUT THE AUTHOR

LAURA DOYLE, author of *The Surrendered Wife* and *The Surrendered Single,* is a full-time relationship coach. She lectures and leads workshops nationwide, and licenses her popular seminars. For workshop information visit www.superwomansolution.com.

Prior to writing *The Surrendered Wife,* Doyle enjoyed a successful career as a marketing copywriter. She is a graduate with honors from San Jose State University's journalism department.

Doyle lives in Southern California with her husband.

Printed in the United States
By Bookmasters